Microsoft® Word 2002
Illustrated Brief

Jennifer A. Duffy

COURSE
TECHNOLOGY
™
THOMSON LEARNING

Australia • Canada • Mexico • Singapore • Spain • United Kingdom • United States

COURSE TECHNOLOGY
THOMSON LEARNING

Microsoft Word 2002 - Illustrated Brief

Jennifer A. Duffy

Managing Editor:
Nicole Jones Pinard

Product Manager:
Emily Heberlein

Associate Product Manager:
Emeline Elliott

Production Editor:
Aimee Poirier

Developmental Editor:
Pamela Conrad

Editorial Assistant:
Christina Kling Garrett

QA Manuscript Reviewers:
John Freitas, Ashlee Welz, Alex White, Harris Bierhoff, Serge Palladino, Holly Schabowski, Jeff Schwartz

Text Designer:
Joseph Lee, Black Fish Design

Composition House:
GEX Publishing Services

Trademarks
Some of the product names and company names used in this book have been used for identification purposes only and may be trademarks or registered trademarks of their respective manufacturers and sellers.

Microsoft and the Office logo are either registered trademarks or trademarks of Microsoft Corporation in the United States and/or other countries. Course Technology is an independent entity from Microsoft Corporation, and not affiliated with Microsoft in any manner.

ISBN 0-619-01899-2

The Illustrated Series Vision

Teaching and writing about computer applications can be extremely rewarding and challenging. How do we engage students and keep their interest? How do we teach them skills that they can easily apply on the job? As we set out to write this book, our goals were to develop a textbook that:

- ▶ works for a beginning student
- ▶ provides varied, flexible and meaningful exercises and projects to reinforce the skills
- ▶ serves as a reference tool
- ▶ makes your job as an educator easier, by providing resources above and beyond the textbook to help you teach your course

Our popular, streamlined format is based on advice from instructional designers and customers. This flexible design presents each lesson on a two-page spread, with step-by-step instructions on the left, and screen illustrations on the right. This signature style, coupled with high-caliber content, provides a comprehensive yet manageable introduction to Microsoft Word 2002 — it is a teaching package for the instructor and a learning experience for the student.

ACKNOWLEDGMENTS

I wish to express particular thanks to Pam Conrad for her tireless help and keen editorial sensibilities. I am also deeply grateful for the support of my husband, Fred Eliot, and our daughter, Isabella, who patiently waited to be born until this book was nearly finished.

Thanks to the reviewers who provided invaluable feedback and ideas to us: Janis Cox and Joe LaMontagne.

Jennifer A. Duffy
and the Illustrated Team

Preface

Welcome to *Microsoft Word 2002–Illustrated Brief.* Each lesson in the book contains elements pictured to the right in the sample two-page spread.

► How is the book organized?

The book is organized into four units on Word, covering creating, editing, and formatting text and documents.

► What kinds of assignments are included in the book? At what level of difficulty?

The lesson assignments use MediaLoft, a fictional chain of bookstore cafés, as the case study. The assignments on the blue pages at the end of each unit increase in difficulty. Project files and case studies, with many international examples, provide a great variety of interesting and relevant business applications for skills. Assignments include:

• **Concepts Reviews** include multiple choice, matching, and screen identification questions.

• **Skills Reviews** provide additional hands-on, step-by-step reinforcement.

• **Independent Challenges** are case projects requiring critical thinking and application of the skills learned in the unit. The Independent Challenges increase in difficulty, with the first Independent Challenge in each unit being the easiest (most step-by-step with detailed instructions). Independent Challenges 2 and 3 become increasingly open-ended, requiring more independent thinking and problem solving.

• **E-Quest Independent Challenges** are case projects with a Web focus. E-Quests require the use of the World Wide Web to conduct research to complete the project.

• **Visual Workshops** show a completed file and require that the file be created without any step-by-step guidance, involving problem solving and an independent application of the unit skills.

Each 2-page spread focuses on a single skill.

Concise text that introduces the basic principles in the lesson and integrates the brief case study (indicated by the paintbrush icon).

Editing Headers and Footers

Unit D
Word 2002

To change header and footer text or to alter the formatting of headers and footers you must first open the Header and Footer areas. You can open headers and footers using the Header and Footer command on the View menu, or by double-clicking a header or footer in Print Layout view. Alice modifies the header by adding a small circle symbol between "Buzz" and the date. She also adds a border under the header text to set it off from the rest of the page. Finally, she removes the header and footer text from the first page of the document.

Steps

Trouble?
If the Header and Footer toolbar is in the way, click its title bar and drag it to a new location.

1. Place the insertion point at the top of page 2, position the ⟂ pointer over the header text at the top of page 2, then double-click
The Header and Footer areas open.

2. Place the insertion point between the two spaces after Buzz, click Insert on the menu bar, then click Symbol
The Symbol dialog box opens and is similar to Figure D-13. Symbols are special characters, such as graphics, shapes, and foreign language characters, that you can insert into a document. The symbols shown in Figure D-13 are the symbols included with the (normal text) font. You can use the Font list arrow on the Symbols tab to view the symbols included with each font on your computer.

3. Scroll the list of symbols if necessary to locate the black circle symbol shown in Figure D-13, select the black circle symbol, click Insert, then click Close
A circle symbol is added at the location of the insertion point.

QuickTip
You can enter different text in the First Page Header and First Page Footer areas.

4. With the insertion point in the header text, click Format on the menu bar, then click Borders and Shading
The Borders and Shading dialog box opens.

TABLE D-3: Buttons on the Header and Footer toolbar

button	function
Insert AutoText ▼	Inserts an AutoText entry, such as a field for the filename, or the author's name
Insert Page Number	Inserts a field for the page number so that the pages are numbered automatically
Insert Number of Pages	Inserts a field for the total number of pages in the document
Format Page Number	Opens the Page Number Format dialog box; use to change the numbering format or to begin automatic page numbering with a specific number
Insert Date	Inserts a field for the current date
Insert Time	Inserts a field for the current time
Page Setup	Opens the Page Setup dialog box
Switch Between Header and Footer	Moves the insertion point between the Header and Footer areas

Hints as well as troubleshooting advice, right where you need it — next to the step itself.

Quickly accessible summaries of key terms, toolbar buttons, or keyboard alternatives connected with the lesson material. Students can refer easily to this information when working on their own projects at a later time.

Every lesson features large, full-color representations of what the screen should look like as students complete the numbered steps.

FIGURE D-13: Symbol dialog box

Black circle symbol is selected

Name of selected symbol

Inserts selected symbol at location of insertion point

The subset changes as you scroll the list of symbols

Available symbols (yours might differ)

Character code for selected symbol

FIGURE D-14: Symbol and border added to header

Dotted line border added to header

Symbol inserted in header

CLUES TO USE

Inserting and creating AutoText entries

In addition to inserting AutoText entries into headers and footers, you can use the AutoText command on the Insert menu to insert AutoText entries into any part of a document. Word includes a number of built-in AutoText entries, including salutations and closings for letters, as well as information for headers and footers. To insert a built-in AutoText entry at the location of the insertion point, point to AutoText on the Insert menu, point to a category on the AutoText menu, then click the AutoText entry you want to insert. You can also use the Insert AutoText button on the Header and Footer toolbar to insert an AutoText entry from the Header/Footer category into a header or footer.

Word's AutoText feature also allows you to store text and graphics that you use frequently so that you can easily insert them in a document. To create a custom AutoText entry, enter the text or graphic you want to store—such as a company name or logo—in a document, select it, point to AutoText on the Insert menu, and then click New. In the Create AutoText dialog box, type a name for your AutoText entry, then click OK. The text or graphic is saved as a custom AutoText entry. To insert a custom AutoText entry in a document, point to AutoText on the Insert menu, click AutoText, select the entry name on the AutoText tab in the AutoCorrect dialog box, click Insert, then click OK.

Clues to Use boxes provide concise information that either expands on the major lesson skill or describes an independent task that in some way relates to the major lesson skill.

The pages are numbered according to unit. D indicates the unit, 13 indicates the page.

► What online content solutions are available to accompany this book?

Visit www.course.com for more information on our online content for Illustrated titles. Options include:

MyCourse.com

Need a quick, simple tool to help you manage your course? Try MyCourse.com, the easiest to use, most flexible syllabus and content management tool available. MyCourse.com offers you brand new content, including Topic Reviews, Extra Case Projects, and Quizzes, to accompany this book.

WebCT

Course Technology and WebCT have partnered to provide you with the highest quality online resources and Web-based tools for your class. Course Technology offers content for this book to help you create your WebCT class, such as a suggested Syllabus, Lecture Notes, Practice Test questions, and more.

Blackboard

Course Technology and Blackboard have also partnered to provide you with the highest quality online resources and Web-based tools for your class. Course Technology offers content for this book to help you create your Blackboard class, such as a suggested Syllabus, Lecture Notes, Practice Test questions, and more.

Instructor Resources

The Instructor's Resource Kit (IRK) CD is Course Technology's way of putting the resources and information needed to teach and learn effectively into your hands. All the components are available on the IRK, (pictured below), and many of the resources can be downloaded from www.course.com.

ASSESSING YOUR STUDENTS

Solution Files
Solution Files are Project Files completed with comprehensive sample answers. Use these files to evaluate your students' work. Or distribute them electronically or in hard copy so students can verify their own work.

ExamView
ExamView is a powerful testing software package that allows you to create and administer printed, computer (LAN-based), and Internet exams. ExamView includes hundreds of questions that correspond to the topics covered in this text, enabling students to generate detailed study guides that include page references for further review. The computer-based and Internet testing components allow students to take exams at their computers, and also save you time by grading each exam automatically.

PRESENTING YOUR CLASS

Figure Files
Figure Files contain all the figures from the book in .jpg format. Use the figure files to create transparency masters or in a PowerPoint presentation.

STUDENT TOOLS

Project Files and Project Files List
To complete most of the units in this book, your students will need **Project Files**. Put them on a file server for students to copy. The Project Files are available on the Instructor's Resource Kit CD-ROM, the Review Pack, and can also be downloaded from www.course.com.

Instruct students to use the **Project Files List** at the end of the book. This list gives instructions on copying and organizing files.

PLANNING YOUR CLASS

Instructor's Manual
Available as an electronic file, the Instructor's Manual is quality-assurance tested and includes unit overviews, detailed lecture topics for each unit with teaching tips, comprehensive sample solutions to all lessons and end-of-unit material, and extra Independent Challenges. The Instructor's Manual is available on the Instructor's Resource Kit CD-ROM, or you can download it from www.course.com.

Sample Syllabus
Prepare and customize your course easily using this sample course outline (available on the Instructor's Resource Kit CD-ROM).

SAM, Skills Assessment Manager for Microsoft Office XP
SAM is the most powerful Office XP assessment and reporting tool that will help you gain a true understanding of your students' proficiency in Microsoft Word, Excel, Access, and PowerPoint 2002. (Available separately from the IRK CD.)

TOM, Training Online Manager for Microsoft Office XP
TOM is Course Technology's MOUS-approved training tool for Microsoft Office XP. Available via the World Wide Web and CD-ROM, TOM allows students to actively learn Office XP concepts and skills by delivering realistic practice through both guided and self-directed simulated instruction.

Contents

Contents

Read This Before You Begin

Software Information and Required Installation

This book was written and tested using Microsoft Office XP - Professional Edition, with a typical installation on Microsoft Windows 2000, with Internet Explorer 5.0 or higher.

What are Project Files?

To complete many of the units in this book, you need to use Project Files. You use a Project File, which contains a partially completed document used in an exercise, so you don't have to type in all the information you need in the document.Your instructor will either provide you with a copy of the Project Files or ask you to make your own copy. Detailed instructions on how to organize your files, as well as a complete listing of all the files you'll need and will create, can be found in the back of the book (look for the yellow pages) in the Project Files List.

Why is my screen different from the book?

1. Your Desktop components and some dialog box options might be different if you are using an operating system other than Windows 2000

2. Depending on your computer hardware capabilities and the Windows Display settings on your computer, you may notice the following differences:
* Your screen may look larger or smaller because of your screen resolution (the height and width of your screen)
* The colors of the title bar in your screen may be a solid blue

3. Depending on your Office settings, your toolbars may display on a single row and your menus may display with a shortened list of frequently used commands. Office menus and toolbars can modify themselves to your working style by displaying only the most frequently used buttons and menu commands.

To view buttons not currently displayed, click a Toolbar Options button ⏷ at the end of either the Standard or Formatting toolbar. To view the full list of menu commands, click the double arrow at the bottom of the menu.

In order to have your toolbars display on two rows, showing all buttons, and to have the full menus display, you must turn off the personalized menus and toolbars feature. Click Tools on the menu bar, Click Customize, select the show Standard and Formatting toolbars on two rows and Always show full menus check boxes on the Options tab, then click Close. This book assumes you are displaying toolbars on two rows and full menus.

Getting
Started with Word 2002

Objectives

► **Understand word processing software**
► **Start Word 2002**
► **Explore the Word program window**
► **Start a document**
⌐MOUS⌐ ► **Save a document**
⌐MOUS⌐ ► **Print a document**
► **Use the Help system**
► **Close a document and exit Word**

Microsoft Word 2002 is a word processing program that makes it easy to create a variety of professional-looking documents, from simple letters and memos to newsletters, research papers, Web pages, business cards, resumes, financial reports, and other documents that include multiple pages of text and sophisticated formatting. In this unit, you will explore Word's editing and formatting features and learn how to start Word and create a document. ✐ Alice Wegman is the marketing manager at MediaLoft, a chain of bookstore cafés that sells books, music, and videos. Alice familiarizes herself with Word and uses it to create a memo to the marketing staff. You will work with Alice as she creates her memo.

Understanding Word Processing Software

A **word processing program** is a software program that includes tools for entering, editing, and formatting text and graphics. Microsoft Word is a powerful word processing program that allows you to create and enhance a wide range of documents quickly and easily. Figure A-1 shows the first page of a report created using Word and illustrates some of the Word features you can use to enhance your documents. The electronic files you create using Word are called **documents**. One of the benefits of using Word is that document files are stored on a disk, making them easy to transport and revise. Alice needs to write a memo to the marketing staff to inform them of an upcoming meeting. Before beginning her memo, she explores Word's editing and formatting capabilities.

You can use Word to accomplish the following tasks:

► Type and edit text
Word's editing tools make it simple to insert and delete text in a document. You can add text to the middle of an existing paragraph, replace text with other text, undo an editing change, and correct typing, spelling, and grammatical errors with ease.

► Copy and move text from one location to another
Using Word's more advanced editing features you can copy or move text from one location and insert it in a different location in a document. You also can copy and move text between documents. Being able to copy and move text means you don't have to retype text that is already entered in a document.

► Format text and paragraphs with fonts, colors, and other elements
Word's sophisticated formatting tools allow you to make the text in your documents come alive. You can change the size, style, and color of text, add lines and shading to paragraphs, and enhance lists with bullets and numbers. Using text-formatting features creatively helps you highlight important ideas in your documents.

► Format and design pages
Word's page-formatting features give you power to design attractive newsletters, create powerful resumes, and produce documents such as business cards, CD labels, and books. You can change the paper size and orientation of your documents, add headers and footers to pages, organize text in columns, and control the layout of text and graphics on each page of a document.

► Enhance documents with tables, charts, diagrams, and graphics
Using Word's powerful graphic tools you can spice up your documents with pictures, photographs, lines, shapes, and diagrams. You also can illustrate your documents with tables and charts to help convey your message in a visually interesting way.

► Create Web pages
Word's Web page design tools allow you to create documents that others can read over the Internet or an intranet. You can enhance Web pages with themes and graphics, add hyperlinks, create online forms, and preview Web pages in your Web browser.

► Use Mail Merge to create form letters and mailing labels
The Word Mail Merge feature allows you to easily send personalized form letters to many different people. You can also use Mail Merge to create mailing labels, directories, e-mail messages, and many other types of documents.

Format the size and appearance of text

Insert graphics

Create columns of text

Add bullets to lists

Create tables

Add headers to every page

Align text in paragraphs evenly

Add lines

Create charts

Add page numbers

MediaLoft Book Buyer Survey

In an effort to develop an economic profile of the MediaLoft book buyers, the marketing department hired the market research firm Takeshita Consultants, Inc. to create and administer a survey of the MediaLoft customer base. A secondary goal of the survey was to identify the areas in which MediaLoft can improve its service and products in the book department. Over 20,000 people completed the survey, which was distributed at MediaLoft stores, the Chicago Book Fair, the Modern Language Association annual meeting, the San Diego Literary Festival, and other events.

Book-buyer Profile

A typical MediaLoft book-buyer is a 42-year-old professional with an annual household income between $40,000 and $60,000. He or she has graduated from college and has one child. The typical book-buyer works in the city and owns a home in an urban or suburban area.

- 42% graduated from college.
- 32% have a graduate level degree.
- 26% have completed high school.
- 60% earn more than $40,000 per year.
- 8% earn more than $70,000 per year.
- 60% are employed as professionals.
- 20% work in clerical/service industries.
- 20% work in trades.

Survey Methods

The survey was distributed to purchasing and non-purchasing customers at MediaLoft stores during January and February 2003. Surveys were distributed at other events as they were held. The table below shows the distribution of surveys by location and by sex. Roughly equal numbers of surveys were completed at the eight MediaLoft stores.

Survey Location	Male	Female
MediaLoft stores	6,657	7,801
Chicago Book Fair	1,567	1,238
MLA annual meeting	563	442
SD Literary Festival	398	487
Other	865	622
Total	10,050	10,590
	Grand Total	20,640

Purchasing Habits

Respondents report they purchase one or two books a month. 80% purchase books online, but 68% prefer to shop for reading material in bookstores.

Preferred Genres

14% 25% 18% 19% 8% 16%

- Fiction
- Biography/Memoir
- Professional
- Non-Fiction
- Technical
- Children's

Customer Satisfaction

On the whole, MediaLoft book customers gave the book department a favorable review. Customers rated the quality of book offerings as excellent, the quantity of titles as very good, and the subject coverage as excellent. Equally favorable ratings were given to the sales staff and the physical appearance of MediaLoft stores. Book-buyers did express interest in seeing a wider selection of non-fiction titles and deeper discounts for computer and professional titles. The organization and variety of titles in the children's and juvenile departments could also be improved.

1 ▶

Word 2002

Planning a document

Before you create a new document, it's a good idea to spend time planning it. Identify the message you want to convey, the audience for your document, and the elements, such as tables or charts, you want to include. You should also think about how you want your document to sound and look—is it a business letter, which should be written in a pleasant, but serious tone and have a formal appearance, or are you creating a flyer that must be colorful, eye-catching, and fun to read?

The purpose and audience for your document will determine the appropriate design. Planning the layout and design of a document involves deciding how to organize the text, selecting the fonts to use, identifying the graphics to include, and selecting the formatting elements that will enhance its message and appeal. For longer documents, such as newsletters, it can be useful to sketch the layout and design of each page before you begin.

Starting Word 2002

Before starting Word, you must start Windows by turning on your computer. Once Windows is running, you can start Word or any other application by using the Start button on the Windows taskbar. You can also start Word by clicking the Word icon on the Windows desktop or the Word icon on the Microsoft Office Shortcut bar, if those items are available on your computer. Alice uses the Start button to start Word so she can familiarize herself with its features.

1. Click the **Start button** 🏁Start on the Windows taskbar

   The Start menu opens on the desktop.

2. Point to **Programs** on the Start menu

   The Programs menu opens, as shown in Figure A-2. The Programs menu displays the list of programs installed on your computer. If you are using personalized menus in Windows, your Programs menu might display only the most frequently used programs; click the double arrow at the bottom of the Programs menu to expand the menu and display the complete list of programs.

Trouble?
If Microsoft Word is not on your Programs menu, ask your technical support person for assistance.

3. Click **Microsoft Word** on the Programs menu

   The **Word program window** opens and displays a blank document and the New Document task pane, as shown in Figure A-3. The blank document opens in the most recently used view. **Views** are different ways of displaying a document in the document window. Figure A-3 shows a blank document in Print Layout view. The lessons in this unit will use Print Layout view.

4. Click the **Print Layout View button** 🔲 as shown in Figure A-3

   If your blank document opened in a different view, the view changes to Print Layout view.

Trouble?
If your toolbars are on one row, click the Toolbar Options button » at the end of the Formatting toolbar, then click Show Buttons on Two Rows.

5. Click the **Zoom list arrow** on the Standard toolbar as shown in Figure A-3, then click **Page Width**

   The blank document fills the document window. Your screen should now match Figure A-3. The blinking vertical line in the upper-left corner of the document window is the **insertion point**. It indicates where text will appear when you type.

6. Move the mouse pointer around in the Word program window

   The mouse pointer changes shape depending on where it is in the Word program window. In the document window in Print Layout view, the mouse pointer changes to an **I-beam pointer** I or a **click and type pointer** I≡. You use these pointers to move the insertion point in the document or to select text to edit. Table A-1 describes common mouse pointers.

7. Place the mouse pointer over a toolbar button

   When you place the pointer over a button or some other element of the Word program window, a ScreenTip appears. A **ScreenTip** is a label that identifies the name of the button or feature.

TABLE A-1: Common Word pointers

pointer	use to
I	Move the insertion point in a document or to select text
I≡ or I≣	Move the insertion point in a blank area of a document in Print Layout or Web Layout view; automatically applies the paragraph formatting required to position text at that location in the document
⌖	Click a button, menu command, or other element of the Word program window; appears when you point to elements of the Word program window
⟋	Select a line or lines of text; appears when you point to the left edge of a line of text in the document window
🖑	Open a hyperlink; appears when you point to a hyperlink in the task pane or a document

FIGURE A-2: Starting Word from the Programs menu

Displays menu of programs installed on your computer

Start button

Click to start Word

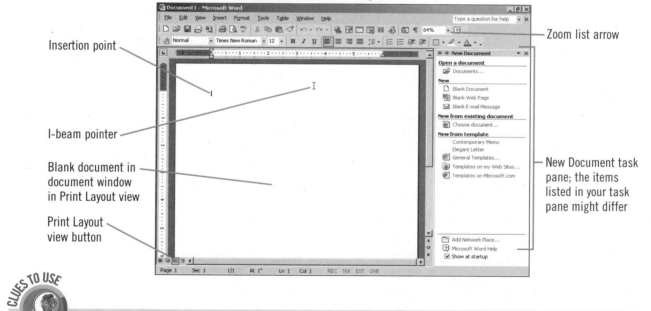

FIGURE A-3: Word program window in Print Layout view

Zoom list arrow

Insertion point

I-beam pointer

Blank document in document window in Print Layout view

Print Layout view button

New Document task pane; the items listed in your task pane might differ

CLUES TO USE

Using Word document views

Each Word view provides features that are useful for working on different types of documents. The default view, Print Layout view, displays a document as it will look on a printed page. Print Layout view is helpful for formatting text and pages, including adjusting document margins, creating columns of text, inserting graphics, and formatting headers and footers. Also useful is Normal view, which shows a simplified layout of a document, without margins, headers and footers, or graphics. When you want to quickly type, edit, and format text, it's often easiest to work in Normal view. Web Layout view allows you to accurately format Web pages or documents that will be

viewed on a computer screen. In Web Layout view, a document appears just as it will when viewed with a Web browser. Finally, Outline view is useful for editing and formatting longer documents that include multiple headings. Outline view allows you to reorganize text by moving the headings.

You switch between views by clicking the view buttons on the horizontal scroll bar or by using the commands on the View menu. Changing views does not affect how the printed document will appear. It simply changes the way you view the document in the document window.

Exploring the Word Program Window

When you start Word, a blank document appears in the document window and the New Document task pane appears. Alice examines the elements of the Word program window.

Using Figure A-4 as a guide, find the elements described below in your program window.

▶ The **title bar** displays the name of the document and the name of the program. Until you give a new document a different name, its temporary name is Document1. The title bar also contains resizing buttons and the program Close button, common to all Windows programs.

▶ The **menu bar** contains the names of the Word menus. Clicking a menu name opens a list of commands from which you can choose. The menu bar also contains the Ask a Question box and the Close Window button. You use the **Ask a Question box** to access the Word Help system.

▶ The **toolbars** contain buttons for the most commonly used commands. The **Standard toolbar** contains buttons for frequently used operating and editing commands, such as saving a document, printing a document, and cutting, copying, and pasting text. The **Formatting toolbar** contains buttons for commonly used formatting commands, such as changing font type and size, applying bold to text, and changing paragraph alignment. The Clues to Use in this lesson provides more information about working with Word's toolbars.

▶ The **New Document task pane** contains shortcuts for opening a document and for creating new documents. The blue words in the New Document task pane are **hyperlinks** that provide quick access to existing documents, document templates, and dialog boxes used for creating and opening documents. As you learn more about Word, you will work with other task panes that provide shortcuts to Word formatting and editing features. Clicking a hyperlink in a task pane can be quicker than using menu commands and toolbar buttons to accomplish a task.

▶ The **document window** displays the current document. You enter text and format your document in the document window.

▶ The horizontal and vertical rulers appear in the document window in Print Layout view. The **horizontal ruler** displays left and right document margins as well as the tab settings and paragraph indents, if any, for the paragraph in which the insertion point is located. The **vertical ruler** displays the top and bottom document margins.

▶ The **vertical and horizontal scroll bars** are used to display different parts of the document in the document window. The scroll bars include **scroll boxes** and **scroll arrows**, which you can use to easily move through a document.

▶ The **view buttons** at the left end of the horizontal scroll bar allow you to display the document in Normal, Web Layout, Print Layout, or Outline view.

▶ The **status bar** displays the page number and section number of the current page, the total number of pages in the document, and the position of the insertion point in inches, lines, and characters. The status bar also indicates the on/off status of several Word features, including tracking changes, overtype mode, and spelling and grammar checking.

FIGURE A-4: Elements of the Word program window

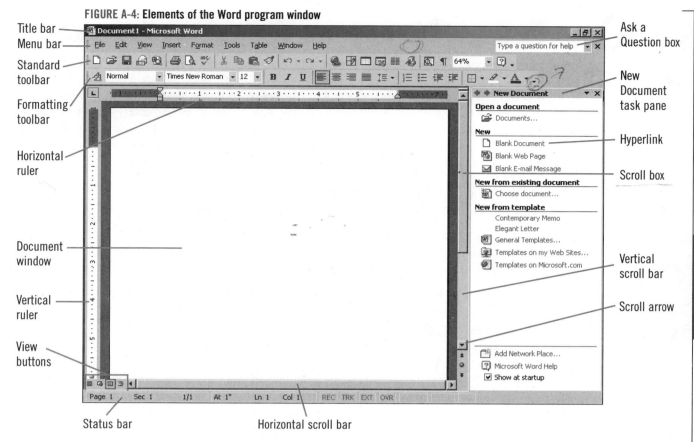

Title bar
Menu bar
Standard toolbar
Formatting toolbar
Horizontal ruler
Document window
Vertical ruler
View buttons
Status bar
Horizontal scroll bar

Ask a Question box
New Document task pane
Hyperlink
Scroll box
Vertical scroll bar
Scroll arrow

CLUES TO USE

Working with toolbars and menus in Word 2002

The lessons in this book assume you are working with full menus and toolbars visible, which means the Standard and Formatting toolbars appear on two rows and display all the buttons, and the menus display the complete list of menu commands.

You can also set Word to use personalized toolbars and menus that modify themselves to your working style. When you use personalized toolbars, the Standard and Formatting toolbars appear on the same row and display only the most frequently used buttons. To use a button that is not visible on a toolbar, click the Toolbar Options button [»] at the end of the toolbar, and then click the button you want on the Toolbar Options list. As you work, Word adds the

buttons you use to the visible toolbars, and moves the buttons you haven't used recently to the Toolbar Options list. Similarly, Word menus adjust to your work habits, so that the commands you use most often appear on shortened menus. You click the double arrow at the bottom of a menu to view additional menu commands.

To work with full toolbars and menus visible, you must turn off the personalized toolbars and menus features. To turn off personalized toolbars and menus, click Tools on the menu bar, click Customize, select the Show Standard and Formatting toolbars on two rows and Always show full menus check boxes on the Options tab, and then click Close.

Word 2002

Starting a Document

You begin a new document by simply typing text in a blank document in the document window. Typing with a word processor is easy because word processors include a **word-wrap** feature, which means as you reach the edge of the page when you type, Word automatically moves the insertion point to the next line of the document. You need only press [Enter] when you want to start a new paragraph or insert a blank line. Also, you can easily edit text in a document by inserting new text or by deleting existing text. ✎ Alice types a quick memo to the marketing staff to inform them of the agenda and schedule for the next marketing meeting.

Steps 123⁴

1. **Click the Close button in the New Document task pane**
The task pane closes and the blank document fills the screen.

2. **Type Memorandum, then press [Enter] four times**
Each time you press [Enter] the insertion point moves to the start of the next line.

3. **Type DATE:, then press [Tab] twice**
Pressing [Tab] moves the insertion point several spaces to the right. You can use the [Tab] key to align the text in a memo header or to indent the first line of a paragraph.

4. **Type April 21, 2003, then press [Enter]**
When you press [Enter], a purple dotted line appears under the date. This dotted underline is a **smart tag**. It indicates that Word recognizes the text as a date. If you move the mouse pointer over the smart tag, a **Smart Tag Actions button** ⓘ appears above the date. Smart tags are just one of many automatic features you will encounter as you type. Table A-2 describes other automatic features available in Word. You can ignore the smart tags in your memo.

5. **Type: TO: [Tab] [Tab] Marketing Staff [Enter]**
     FROM: [Tab] Your Name [Enter]
     RE: [Tab] [Tab] Marketing Meeting [Enter] [Enter]
Red or green wavy lines may appear under the words you typed. A red, wavy line means the word is not in Word's dictionary and might be misspelled. A green, wavy line indicates a possible grammar error. You can correct any typing errors you make later.

6. **Type The next marketing meeting will be held May 6th at 10 a.m. in the Bloomsbury room on the ground floor.**
As you type, notice that the insertion point moves automatically to the next line of the document. You also might notice that Word corrects typing errors or makes typographical adjustments as you type. This feature is called **AutoCorrect**. AutoCorrect automatically detects and adjusts typos, certain misspelled words (such as "taht" for "that"), and incorrect capitalization as you type. For example, in the memo, Word automatically changed "6th" to "6th."

7. **Type Heading the agenda will be a discussion of our new cafe music series, scheduled for August. Please bring ideas for promoting this exciting new series to the meeting.**
When you type the first few characters of "August," Word's AutoComplete feature displays the complete word in a ScreenTip. **AutoComplete** suggests text to insert quickly into your documents. You can ignore AutoComplete for now. Your memo should resemble Figure A-5.

8. **Position the pointer I after for (but before the space) in the second sentence, then click**
Clicking moves the insertion point after "for."

9. **Press [Backspace] three times, then type to debut in**
Pressing [Backspace] removes the character before the insertion point.

10. **Move the insertion point before marketing in the first sentence, then press [Delete] ten times to remove the word marketing and the space after it**
Pressing [Delete] removes the character after the insertion point. Figure A-6 shows the revised memo.

QuickTip
If you press the wrong key, press [Backspace] to erase the mistake, then try again.

QuickTip
Smart tags and other automatic feature markers appear on screen, but do not print.

QuickTip
To reverse an AutoCorrect adjustment, immediately click the Undo button ↺ on the Standard toolbar.

QuickTip
Type just one space after a period at the end of a sentence when typing with a word processor.

FIGURE A-5: Memo text in the document window

Blank lines between paragraphs

Purple dotted underline indicates a smart tag

Red, wavy underline indicates a possible misspelled word (your memo will show your name)

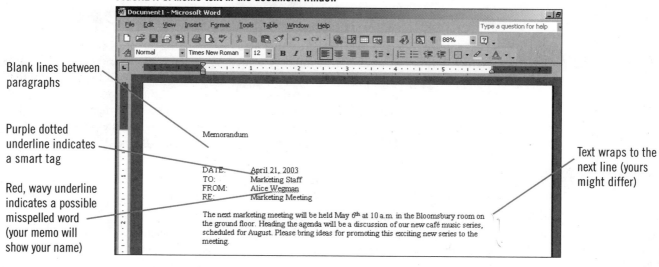

Text wraps to the next line (yours might differ)

FIGURE A-6: Edited memo text

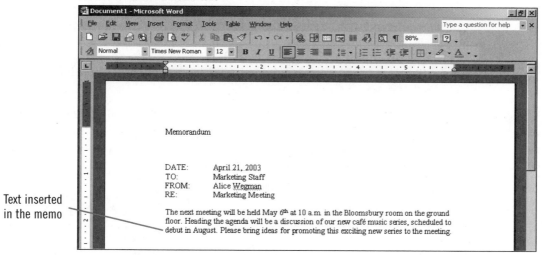

Text inserted in the memo

TABLE A-2: Word's automatic features

feature	what appears	to use
AutoComplete	A ScreenTip suggesting text to insert appears as you type	Press [Enter] to insert the text suggested by the ScreenTip; continue typing to reject the suggestion
Spelling and grammar	A red, wavy line under a word indicates a possible misspelling; a green wavy line under text indicates a possible grammatical error	Right-click red- or green-underlined text to display a shortcut menu of correction options; click a correction to accept it and remove the wavy underline
AutoCorrect	A small blue box appears when you place the pointer under text corrected by AutoCorrect; an AutoCorrect Options button appears when you point to the corrected text	Word automatically corrects typos, minor spelling errors, and capitalization, and adds typographical symbols (such as © and ™) as you type; to reverse an AutoCorrect adjustment, click the AutoCorrect Options button, then click Undo
Smart tag	A purple dotted line appears under text Word recognizes as a date, name, address, or place; a Smart Tag Actions button appears when you point to a smart tag	Click the Smart Tag Actions button to display a shortcut menu of options (such as adding a name to your address book in Outlook or opening your Outlook calendar to a date); to remove a smart tag, click Remove this Smart Tag on the shortcut menu

Saving a Document

Word 2002

To store a document permanently so you can open and edit it in the future, you must save a document as a **file** on your computer. When you **save** a document you give it a name, called a **filename**, and indicate the location where you want to store the file. Files can be saved to your computer's internal hard disk, to a floppy disk, or to a variety of other locations. You can save a document using the Save button on the Standard toolbar or the Save command on the File menu. Once you have saved a document for the first time, you should save it again every few minutes and always before printing so that the saved file is updated to reflect your latest changes. 🖋 Alice saves her memo with the filename Marketing Memo.

Steps

[handwritten: SAVE 6 steps 3 ng]

Trouble?

If you don't see the extension .doc on the filenames in the Save As dialog box, don't worry. Windows can be set to display or not to display the file extensions.

Trouble?

This book assumes your Project Files are stored in drive A. Substitute the correct drive or folder if this is not the case.

1. Click the **Save button** 💾 on the Standard toolbar

The first time you save a document, the Save As dialog box opens, as shown in Figure A-7. The default filename, Memorandum, appears in the File name text box. The default filename is based on the first few words of the document. The ".doc" extension is assigned automatically to all Word documents to distinguish them from files created in other software programs. To save the document with a different filename, type a new filename in the File name text box, and use the Save in list arrow to select where you want to store the document file. You do not need to type .doc when you type a new filename. Table A-3 describes the functions of the buttons in the Save As dialog box.

2. Type **Marketing Memo** in the File name text box

The new filename replaces the default filename. It's a good idea to give your documents brief filenames that describe the contents.

3. Click the **Save in list arrow**, then navigate to the drive or folder where your Project Files are located

The drive or folder where your Project Files are located appears in the Save in list box. Your Save As dialog box should resemble Figure A-8.

4. Click **Save**

The document is saved to the location you specified in the Save As dialog box, and the title bar displays the new filename, "Marketing Memo."

5. Place the insertion point before **August** in the second sentence, type **early**, then press **[Spacebar]**

You can continue to work on a document after you have saved it with a new filename.

6. Click 💾

Your change to the memo is saved. Saving a document after you give it a filename saves the changes you make to a document. You also can click File on the menu bar, and then click Save to save a document.

CLUES TO USE

Recovering lost document files

Sometimes while you are working on a document, Word might freeze, making it impossible to continue working, or you might experience a power failure that shuts down your computer. Should this occur, Word has a built-in recovery feature that allows you to open and save the files that were open during the interruption. When you restart Word after an interruption, the Document Recovery task pane opens on the left side of your screen and lists both the original and the recovered versions of the Word files. If you're not sure which file to open (original or recovered), it's usually better to open the recovered file because it includes your latest changes to the document. You can, however, open and review all the versions of the file that were recovered and select the best one to save. Each file listed in the Document Recovery task pane has a list arrow with options that allow you to open the file, save the file, delete the file, or show repairs made to the file.

FIGURE A-7: Save As dialog box

Active folder or drive

Folders and files in the active folder or drive (yours will differ)

Default filename and file extension are selected

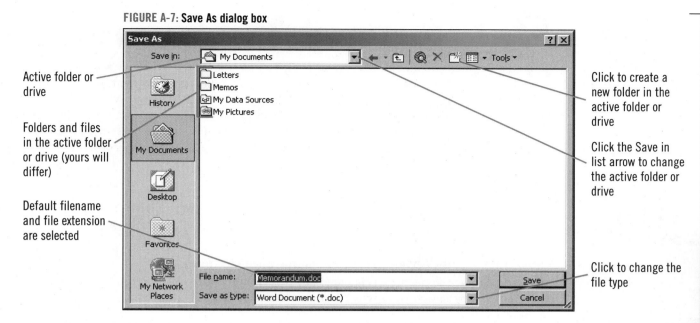

Click to create a new folder in the active folder or drive

Click the Save in list arrow to change the active folder or drive

Click to change the file type

FIGURE A-8: File to be saved to drive A

Location of Project Files (yours might differ)

New filename

Your dialog box might list the files and folders in the active drive or folder here

TABLE A-3: Save As dialog box buttons

button	use to
⬅ **Back**	Navigate to the drive or folder previously shown in the Save in list box; click the Back list arrow to navigate to a recently displayed drive or folder
🔼 **Up One Level**	Navigate to the next highest level in the folder hierarchy (to the drive or folder that contains the current folder)
🔍 **Search the Web**	Connect to the World Wide Web to locate a folder or file
✖ **Delete**	Delete the selected folder or file
📁 **Create New Folder**	Create a new folder in the current folder or drive
▦ ▾ **Views**	Change the way folder and file information is shown in the Save As dialog box
Tools ▾ **Tools**	Open a menu of commands related to the selected drive, folder, or file

Word 2002

Printing a Document

Before you print a document, it's a good habit to examine it in Print Preview to see what it will look like when printed. When you are ready, you can print a document using the Print button on the Standard toolbar or the Print command on the File menu. When you use the Print button, the document prints using the default print settings. If you want to print more than one copy of a document or select other printing options, you must use the Print command. ✎ Alice displays her memo in Print Preview and then prints a copy.

Steps

1. **Click the Print Preview button** 🔍 **on the Standard toolbar**
   The document appears in Print Preview. It is useful to examine a document carefully in Print Preview so that you can correct any problems before printing it.

QuickTip

You can also use the Zoom list arrow on the Print Preview toolbar to change the magnification in the Print Preview window.

2. **Move the pointer over the memo text until it changes to** 🔍, **then click the memo**
   Clicking with the 🔍 pointer magnifies the document in the Print Preview window and changes the pointer to 🔍. The memo appears in the Print Preview window exactly as it will look when printed, as shown in Figure A-9. Clicking with 🔍 reduces the size of the document in the Print Preview window.

3. **Click the Magnifier button** 🔍 **on the Print Preview toolbar**
   Clicking the Magnifier button turns off the magnification feature and allows you to edit the document in Print Preview. In edit mode, the pointer changes to I. The Magnifier button is a **toggle button**, which means you can use it to switch back and forth between magnification mode and edit mode.

4. **Compare the text on your screen with the text in Figure A-9, examine your memo carefully for typing or spelling errors, correct any mistakes, then click the Close Preview button** Close **on the Print Preview toolbar**
   Print Preview closes and the memo appears in the document window.

5. **Click the Save button** 💾 **on the Standard toolbar**
   If you made any changes to the document since you last saved it, the changes are saved.

6. **Click File on the menu bar, then click Print**
   The Print dialog box opens, as shown in Figure A-10. Depending on the printer installed on your computer, your print settings might differ slightly from those in the figure. You can use the Print dialog box to change the current printer, change the number of copies to print, select what pages of a document to print, and modify other printing options.

7. **Click OK**
   The dialog box closes and a copy of the memo prints using the default print settings. You can also click the Print button 🖨 on the Standard toolbar or the Print Preview toolbar to print a document using the default print settings.

FIGURE A-9: Memo in the Print Preview window

Magnifier button

Close Preview button

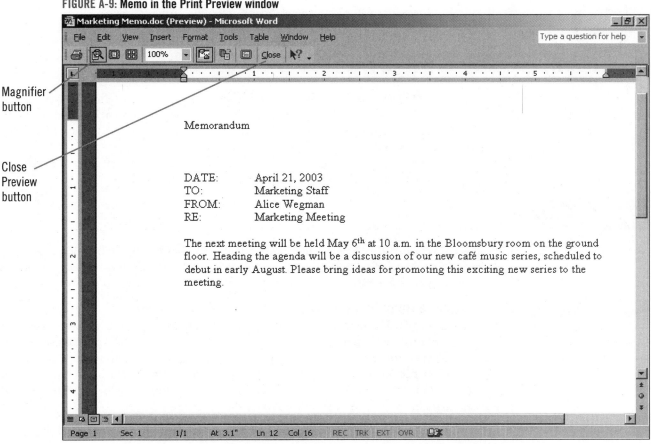

FIGURE A-10: Print dialog box

Default printer (yours might differ)

Change printer properties, such as paper size

Select the pages to print

Change the number of copies to print

Change the number of pages to print on a sheet of paper

Select the aspects of the document to print

Print using current settings

Using the Help System

Word includes an extensive Help system that provides immediate access to definitions, instructions, and useful tips for working with Word. You can quickly access the Help system by typing a question in the Ask a Question box on the menu bar, or by clicking the Microsoft Word Help button on the Standard toolbar. Table A-4 describes the many ways to get help while using Word. ✎ Alice is curious to learn more about typing with AutoCorrect and viewing a document in Print Preview. She searches the Word Help system to discover more about these features.

Steps

1. Type AutoCorrect in the Ask a Question box on the menu bar, then press [Enter]

A drop-down menu of help topics related to AutoCorrect opens. You can select a topic from this menu or click See more… to view additional help topics related to your query.

QuickTip

Click the Print button 🖨 on the Help window toolbar to print the current help topic.

2. Click About automatic corrections on the drop-down menu

The Microsoft Word Help window opens, as shown in Figure A-11. The left pane of the Help window contains the Contents, Answer Wizard, and Index tabs, which you can use to search for and display information on help topics. The right pane of the Help window displays the "About automatic corrections" help topic you selected. The blue text in the Help window indicates a link to a definition or to more information about the topic. Notice that the pointer changes to 🖑 when you move it over the blue text.

3. Read the information in the Help window, then click the blue text hyperlinks

Clicking the link expands the help topic to display more detailed information. A definition of "hyperlink" appears in green text in the Help window.

4. Read the definition, then click hyperlinks again to close the definition

5. Click Using AutoCorrect to correct errors as you type, then read the expanded information, clicking the down scroll arrow as necessary to read the entire help topic

Clicking the up or down scroll arrow allows you to navigate through the help topic when all the text does not fit in the Help window. You can also scroll by clicking the scroll bar above and below the scroll box, or by dragging the scroll box up or down in the scroll bar.

QuickTip

Click the Back ⬅ and Forward ➡ buttons on the Help window toolbar to navigate between the help topics you have viewed.

6. Click the Answer Wizard tab in the left pane if necessary, type print a document in the What would you like to do? text box, then click Search

When you click Search, a list of help topics related to your query appears in the Select topic to display box on the Answer Wizard tab, as shown in Figure A-12. The active help topic— the topic selected in the Select topic to display box—appears in the right pane.

7. Click the Index tab, type print preview in the Type keywords text box, then click Search

As you type, notice that Word automatically supplies possible keywords in the Type keywords box. When you click Search, a list of help topics related to Print Preview appears in the Choose a topic box. You can use the Index tab to narrow the scope of the help topics related to your query by searching for topics related to specific words or phrases.

8. Click Edit text in print preview in the Choose a topic box

The help topic appears in the right pane of the Help window.

9. Click the Close button on the Help window title bar to close Help

FIGURE A-11: Microsoft Word Help window

Prints active help topic

Index tab appears in left pane; your active tab might differ

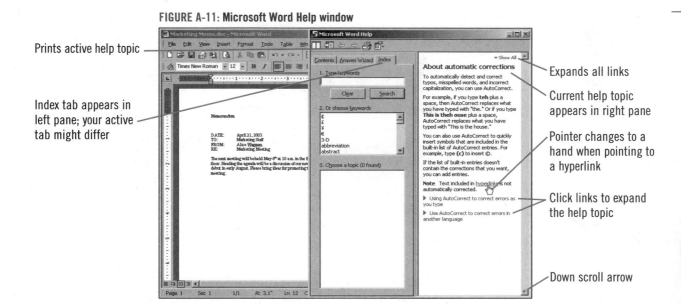

Expands all links

Current help topic appears in right pane

Pointer changes to a hand when pointing to a hyperlink

Click links to expand the help topic

Down scroll arrow

FIGURE A-12: Answer Wizard tab in the Microsoft Word Help window

Query used to search for topic

List of help topics related to query

Close button

Active help topic

TABLE A-4: Word resources for getting Help

resource	function	to use
Ask a Question box	Provides quick access to the Help system	Type a word or question in the Ask a Question box, then press [Enter]
Office Assistant	Displays tips and Help topics related to your current task and provides access to the Help system	Press [F1] or click the Microsoft Word Help button ⚇ on the Standard toolbar, select a Help topic or type a word or question in the Office Assistant dialog box, then click Search
Microsoft Word Help window	Catalogs and displays the detailed Help topics included in the Help system	Browse the table of contents on the Contents tab, type a question in the text box on the Answer Wizard tab, or search for topics related to a keyword on the Index tab
What's This?	Displays information about elements of the Word program window in ScreenTips	Press [Shift][F1] or click the What's This? command on the Help menu, then use the ⩗? pointer to click the element for which you want help
Help on the World Wide Web	Connects to the Microsoft Office Web site, where you can search for information on a topic	Click the Office on the Web command on the Help menu

Closing a Document and Exiting Word

When you finish working on a document and have saved your changes, you can close the document using the Close Window button on the menu bar or the Close command on the File menu. Closing a document closes the document only, it does not close the Word program window. To close the Word program window and exit Word, you can use the Close button on the title bar or the Exit command on the File menu. Using the Exit command closes all open documents. It's good practice to save and close your documents before exiting Word. Figure A-14 shows the Close buttons on the title bar and menu bar. Alice closes the memo and exits Word.

Steps

1. Click File on the menu bar, then click Close

If you saved your changes to the document before closing it, the document closes. If you did not save your changes, an alert box opens asking if you want to save the changes.

QuickTip

Click the New Blank Document button on the Standard toolbar to create a new blank document.

2. Click Yes if necessary

The document closes, but the Word program window remains open, as shown in Figure A-15. You can create or open another document, access Help, or close the Word program window.

3. Click File on the menu bar, then click Exit

The Word program window closes. If any Word documents were still open when you exited Word, Word would close all open documents, prompting you to save changes to those documents if necessary.

Using the Office Assistant to get Help

The **Office Assistant**, shown in Figure A-13, is an animated character that appears on your screen to provide tips while you work. For example, when you begin typing a letter, the Office Assistant anticipates what you are doing and opens to offer help writing a letter. You can accept this help or continue working on your own. The Office Assistant also appears when you use the Microsoft Word Help button ⧆ to access the Word Help system. In this case, the Office Assistant displays a list of help topics related to tasks you have recently completed and provides space for you to search for information on other topics. Selecting a help topic in the Office Assistant displays that topic in the Microsoft Help window. When you finish working with the Office Assistant, right-click it and then click Hide to close it. You also can turn off the Office Assistant: right-click it, click Options, deselect the Use the Office Assistant check box on the Options tab in the Office Assistant dialog box, and then click OK. To turn it on again, click Show Office Assistant on the Help menu.

FIGURE A-13: Office Assistant

FIGURE A-14: Close and Close Window buttons

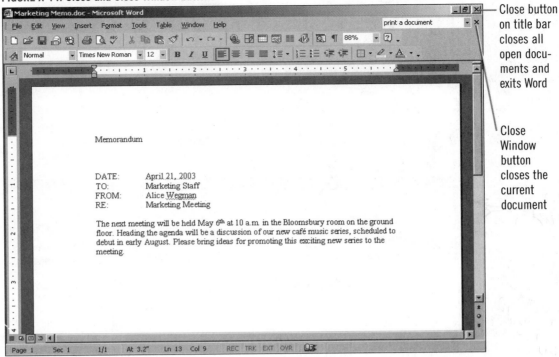

Close button on title bar closes all open documents and exits Word

Close Window button closes the current document

FIGURE A-15: Word program window with no documents open

New Blank Document button

Practice

▶ Concepts Review

Label the elements of the Word program window shown in Figure A-16.

FIGURE A-16

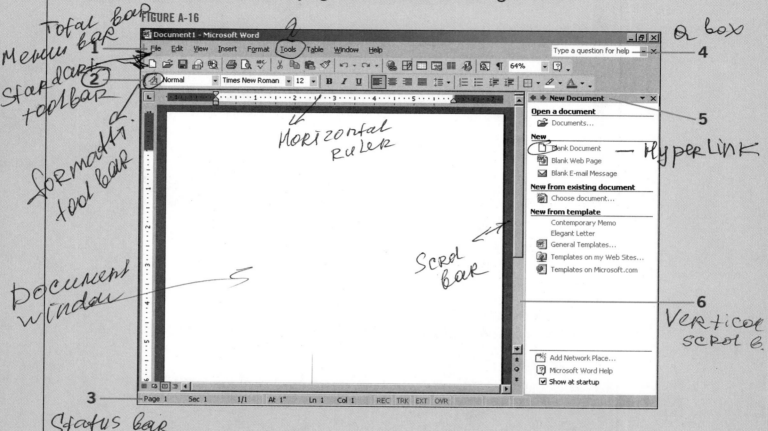

Handwritten annotations:
- Total bar
- Menu bar — 1
- Standard toolbar — 2
- Formatti. tool bar
- Document window
- Horizontal ruler
- Scrol bar
- Q box — 4
- Hyperlink — 5
- Vertical scrol b. — 6
- Status bar — 3

Match each term with the statement that best describes it.

Practbar

- 7. **Print Preview**
- 8. **Office Assistant** *Help.*
- 9. **Status bar**
- 10. **Menu bar**
- 11. **AutoComplete**
- 12. **Horizontal ruler** *pagm*
- 13. **AutoCorrect**
- 14. **Normal view**

- **a.** Suggests text to insert into a document *11*
- **b.** Provides access to Word commands *8*
- **c.** Displays the document exactly as it will look when printed *(7)*
- **d.** Provides tips on using Word and displays Help topics *10*
- **e.** Fixes certain errors as you type *13*
- **f.** Displays the number of pages in the current document *9*
- **g.** Displays a simple layout view of a document *14*
- **h.** Displays tab settings and document margins *14*

Select the best answer from the list of choices.

15. Which element of the Word program window contains hyperlinks to help you quickly accomplish a task?
- **a.** Formatting toolbar
- **b.** Menu bar
- **c.** New Document task pane
- **d.** Status bar

16. Which button is found on the Formatting toolbar?
- **a.** Underline button
- **b.** Drawing button
- **c.** Format Painter button
- **d.** Tables and Borders button

17. What is the function of the Exit command on the File menu?
- **a.** To save changes to and close the current document
- **b.** To close the current document without saving changes
- **c.** To close all open documents and the Word program window
- **d.** To close all open programs

18. Which view would you use if you want to adjust the margins in a document?
- **a.** Outline view
- **b.** Print Layout view
- **c.** Normal view
- **d.** Web Layout view

19. Which of the following does *not* appear on the status bar?
- **a.** The current page number
- **b.** The current line number
- **c.** The Overtype mode status
- **d.** The current tab settings

20. Which of the following is *not* used to access Word Help topics?
- **a.** The Ask a Question box
- **b.** The Search task pane
- **c.** The Office Assistant
- **d.** The Answer Wizard

▶ Skills Review

1. Start Word 2002.
- **a.** Start Word using the Programs menu.
- **b.** Switch to Print Layout view if necessary.
- **c.** Change the zoom level to Page Width if necessary.

2. Explore the Word program window.
- **a.** Identify as many elements of the Word program window as you can without referring to the unit material.
- **b.** Click each menu name on the menu bar and drag the pointer through the menu commands.
- **c.** Point to each button on the Standard and Formatting toolbars and read the ScreenTips.
- **d.** Point to each hyperlink in the New Document task pane.
- **e.** Click the view buttons to view the blank document in Normal, Web Layout, Print Layout, and Outline view.
- **f.** Return to Print Layout view.

3. Start a document.
- **a.** Close the New Document task pane.
- **b.** In a new blank document, begin typing a fax to one of your customers at Plateau Tours and Travel in Montreal.
- **c.** Type **FAX** at the top of the page, then press [Enter] four times.

d. Type the following, pressing [Tab] as indicated and pressing [Enter] at the end of each line:
To: [Tab] **Dr. Monique Lacasse**
From: [Tab] **Your Name**
Date: [Tab] **Today's Date**
Re: [Tab] **Travel arrangements**
Pages: [Tab] **1**
Fax: [Tab] **(514) 555-3948**

e. Press [Enter], then type **I have reserved a space for you on the February 4-18 Costa Rica Explorer tour. You are scheduled to depart Montreal's Dorval Airport on Plateau Tours and Travel charter flight 234 at 7:45 a.m. on February 4th, arriving in San Jose at 4:30 p.m. local time.**

f. Press [Enter] twice, then type **Please call me at (514) 555-4983 or stop by our offices on rue St-Denis.**

g. Insert this sentence at the beginning of the second paragraph: **I must receive full payment within 48 hours to hold your reservation.**

h. Using the [Backspace] key, delete **Travel** in the Re: line, then type **Costa Rica tour.**

i. Using the [Delete] key, delete **48** in the last sentence, then type **72.**

4. Save a document.

a. Click File on the menu bar, then click Save.

b. Save the document as **Lacasse Fax** to the drive and folder where your Project Files are located.

c. After your name, type a comma, a space, and then type **Plateau Tours and Travel.**

d. Click the Save button to save your changes to the document.

5. Print a document.

a. Click the Print Preview button to view the document in Print Preview.

b. Click the word FAX to zoom in on the document, then proofread the fax.

c. Click the Magnifier button to switch to edit mode, then correct any typing errors in your document.

d. Close Print Preview, then save your changes to the document.

e. Print the fax using the default print settings.

6. Use the Help system.

a. Click the Microsoft Word Help button to open the Office Assistant. (*Hint*: If the Help window opens instead of the Office Assistant, close the Help window, click Help on the menu bar, click Show the Office Assistant, then click the Microsoft Word Help button again.)

b. Type **save a document** in the Office Assistant text box, then click Search.

c. Click the topic Save a document.

d. Read about saving documents in Word by clicking the links to expand the help topic.

e. Click the Contents tab, then double-click the topic Viewing and Navigating Documents.

f. Click the topic Zoom in on or out of a document, then read the help topic.

g. Close the Microsoft Word Help window.

7. Close a document and exit Word.

a. Close the Lacasse Fax document, saving your changes if necessary.

b. Exit Word.

▶ Independent Challenge 1

You are a performance artist, well known for your innovative work with computers. The Missoula Arts Council president, Jeb Zobel, has asked you to be the keynote speaker at an upcoming conference in Missoula, Montana, on the role of technology in the arts. You are pleased at the invitation, and write a letter to Mr. Zobel accepting the invitation and confirming the details. Your letter to Mr. Zobel should reference the following information:

- The conference will be held October 10–12, 2003 at the civic center in Missoula.
- You have been asked to speak for one hour on Saturday, October 11, followed by a half hour for questions.
- Mr. Zobel suggested the lecture topic "Technology's Effect on Art and Culture."
- Your talk will include a 20-minute slide presentation.
- The Missoula Arts Council will make your travel arrangements.
- Your preference is to arrive in Missoula on Friday, October 10, and depart on Sunday, October 12.
- You want to fly in and out of the airport closest to your home.

a. Start Word.

b. Save a new blank document as **Zobel Letter** to the drive and folder where your Project Files are located.

c. Model your letter to Mr. Zobel after the sample business letter shown in Figure A-17: there are 3 blank lines after the date, 1 blank line after the inside address, 1 blank line after the salutation, 1 blank line after each body paragraph, and 3 blank lines between the closing and your typed name.

d. Begin the letter by typing today's date.

e. Type the inside address. Be sure to include Mr. Zobel's title and the name of the organization. Make up a street address.

f. Type a salutation.

g. Using the information listed above, type the body of the letter:
- In the first paragraph, accept the invitation to speak and confirm the important conference details.
- In the second paragraph, confirm your lecture topic and provide any relevant details.
- In the third paragraph, state your travel preferences.
- Type a short final paragraph.

h. Type a closing, then include your name in the signature block.

i. Save your changes.

j. Preview and print the letter, then close the document and exit Word.

FIGURE A-17

July 8, 2003

Dr. Amanda Russell
Department of Literature and Creative Writing
Nashua State College
Nashua, NH 03285

Dear Dr. Russell:

Thank you for the invitation to speak at your upcoming seminar on "The Literature of Place." I will be happy to do so. I understand that the seminar will be held from 2:30 p.m. to 4:30 p.m. on September 17 in the Sanders Auditorium. As you suggested, I will address the topic "Writers of the Monadonock Region."

I appreciate your invitation and I look forward to working with you on September 17.

Sincerely,

Jessica Grange

► Independent Challenge 2

Your company has recently installed Word 2002 on its company network. As the training manager it's your responsibility to teach employees how to use the new software productively. Since installing Word 2002, several employees have asked you about smart tags. In response to their queries, you decide to write a memo to all employees and explain how to use the smart tag feature. You know that smart tags are designed to help users perform tasks in Word that normally would require opening a different program, such as Microsoft Outlook (a desktop information-management program that includes e-mail, calendar, and address book features). Before writing your memo, you'll learn more about smart tags by searching the Word Help system.

FIGURE A-18

WORD TRAINING MEMORANDUM

To: All employees
From: Your Name, Training Manager
Date: Today's date
Re: Smart tags in Word 2002

a. Start Word and save a new blank document as **Smart Tags Memo** to the drive and folder where your Project Files are located.

b. Type **WORD TRAINING MEMORANDUM** at the top of the document, press [Enter] four times, then type the memo heading information shown in Figure A-18. Make sure to include your name in the From line and the current date in the Date line.

c. Press [Enter] twice to place the insertion point where you will begin typing the body of your memo.

d. Search the Word Help system for information on working with smart tags.

e. Type your memo after completing your research. In your memo, define smart tags, then explain what they look like, how to use smart tags, and how to remove smart tags from a document.

f. Save your changes, preview and print the memo, then close the document and exit Word.

► Independent Challenge 3

Yesterday you interviewed for a job as marketing director at Komata Web Designs. You spoke with several people at Komata, including Hiro Kobayashi, Director of Operations, whose business card is shown in Figure A-19. You need to write a follow-up letter to Mr. Kobayashi, thanking him for the interview and expressing your interest in the company and the position. He also asked you to send him some samples of your marketing work, which you will enclose with the letter.

FIGURE A-19

a. Start Word and save a new blank document as **Komata Letter** to the drive and folder where your Project Files are located.

b. Begin the letter by typing today's date.

c. Four lines below the date, type the inside address, referring to Figure A-19 for the address information. Be sure to include the recipient's title, company name, and full mailing address in the inside address. (*Hint*: When typing a foreign address, type the name of the country in capital letters by itself on the last line.)

d. Two lines below the inside address, type the salutation.

e. Two lines below the salutation, type the body of the letter according to the following guidelines:
   • In the first paragraph, thank him for the interview. Then restate your interest in the position and express your desire to work for the company. Add any specific details you think will enhance the power of your letter.

- In the second paragraph, note that you are enclosing three samples of your work and explain something about the samples you are enclosing.
- Type a short final paragraph.

f. Two lines below the last body paragraph, type a closing, then four lines below the closing, type the signature block. Be sure to include your name in the signature block.

g. Two lines below the signature block, type an enclosure notation. (*Hint*: An enclosure notation usually includes the word "Enclosures" or the abbreviation "Enc." followed by the number of enclosures in parentheses.)

h. Save your changes.

i. Preview and print the letter, then close the document and exit Word.

 # Independent Challenge 4

Unlike personal letters or many e-mail messages, business letters are formal in tone and format. The World Wide Web is one source for information on writing styles, proper document formatting, and other business etiquette issues. In this independent challenge, you will research guidelines and tips for writing effective and professional business letters. Your online research should seek answers to the following questions: What is important to keep in mind when writing a business letter? What are the parts of a business letter? What are some examples of types of business letters? What are some useful tips for writing business letters?

a. Use your favorite search engine to search the Web for information on writing and formatting business letters. Use the keywords **business letters** to conduct your search. If your search does not result in links to information on business letters, try looking at the following Web sites: www.eHow.com, www.business-letters.com, or www.about.com.

b. Review the Web sites you find. Print at least two Web pages that offer useful guidelines for writing business letters.

c. Start Word and save a new blank document as **Business Letters** to the drive and folder where your Project Files are located.

d. Type your name at the top of the document, then press [Enter] twice.

e. Type a brief report on the results of your research. Your report should answer the following questions:

- What are the URLs of the Web sites you visited to research guidelines for writing a business letter? (*Hint*: A URL is a Web page's address. An example of a URL is www.eHow.com.)
- What is important to keep in mind when writing a business letter?
- What are the parts of a business letter?
- In what situations do people write business letters? Provide as many examples as you can think of.

f. Save your changes to the document, preview and print it, then close the document and exit Word.

Visual Workshop

Create the cover letter shown in Figure A-20. Since you plan to print the letter on your letterhead, you do not need to include your return address. Save the document with the name **Publishing Cover Letter** to the drive and folder where your Project Files are stored, print a copy of the letter, then close the document and exit Word.

FIGURE A-20

June 16, 2003

Ms. Olivia Johansen
Managing Editor
Conway Press
483 Grove Street
Wellesley, MA 02181

Dear Ms. Johansen:

I read of the opening for an editorial assistant on the June 15 edition of Boston.com, and I would like to be considered for the position. A recent graduate of Whitfield College, I am interested in pursuing a career in publishing.

My desire for a publishing career springs from my interest in writing and editing. At Whitfield College, I was a frequent contributor to the student newspaper and was involved in creating a Web site for student poetry and short fiction.

I have a wealth of experience using Microsoft Word in professional settings. For the past several summers I worked as an office assistant for Packer Investment Consultants, where I used Word to create newsletters and financial reports for clients. During the school year, I also worked part-time in the Whitfield College admissions office. Here I used Word's mail merge feature to create form letters and mailing labels.

My enclosed resume details my talents and experience. I would welcome the opportunity to discuss the position and my qualifications with you. I can be reached at 617-555-3849.

Sincerely,

Your Name

Enc.

Editing

Documents

Word's sophisticated editing features make it easy to revise and polish your documents. In this unit, you learn how to open an existing file, revise it by replacing, copying, and moving text, and then save the document as a new file. You also learn to perfect your documents using Word's proofing tools, and to quickly create attractive, professionally designed documents using wizards and templates. ✒ Alice Wegman needs to create a press release about a new MediaLoft lecture series in New York. The press release should provide information about the series so that newspapers, radio stations, and other media outlets can announce it to the public. Alice also needs to create a fax coversheet to use when she faxes the press release to her list of press contacts. You will work with Alice as she creates these documents.

Word 2002

Opening a Document

Sometimes the easiest way to create a document is to edit an existing document and save it with a new filename. To modify a document, you must first **open** it so that it displays in the document window. Word offers several methods for opening documents, described in Table B-1. Once you have opened a file, you can use the Save As command to create a new file that is a copy of the original. You can then edit the new file without making changes to the original. ✎ Rather than write her press release from scratch, Alice decides to modify a press release written for a similar event. She begins by opening the press release document and saving it with a new filename.

Trouble?

If the New Document task pane is not open, click File on the menu bar, then click New.

QuickTip

You also can use the Open button 🖃 on the Standard toolbar or the Open command on the File menu to open the Open dialog box.

QuickTip

You also can double-click a filename in the Open dialog box to open the file.

1. Start **Word**

Word opens and a blank document and the New Document task pane appear in the program window, as shown in Figure B-1. The New Document task pane contains links for opening existing documents and for creating new documents.

2. Click the **Documents** or **More Documents** hyperlink under Open a document in the New Document task pane

The Open dialog box opens. You use the Open dialog box to locate and select the file you want to open. The Look in list box displays the current drive or folder.

3. Click the **Look in list arrow**, then click the **drive** containing your Project Files

A list of Project Files appears in the Open dialog box, as shown in Figure B-2. If your Project Files are located in a folder, double-click the folder to display its contents.

4. Click the filename **WD B-1** in the Open dialog box, then click **Open**

The document opens. Notice that the filename WD B-1 appears in the title bar. Once you have opened a file, you can edit it and use the Save or the Save As command to save your changes. You use the **Save** command when you want to save the changes you make to a file, overwriting the file that is stored on a disk. You use the **Save As** command when you want to create a new file with a different filename, leaving the original file intact.

5. Click **File** on the menu bar, then click **Save As**

The Save As dialog box opens. By saving a file with a new filename, you create a document that is identical to the original document. The original filename is selected (highlighted) in the File name text box. Any text you type will replace the selected text.

6. Type **NY Press Release** in the File name text box, then click **Save**

The original file closes and the NY Press Release file is displayed in the document window. Notice the new filename in the title bar. You can now make changes to the press release file without affecting the original file.

TABLE B-1: Methods for opening documents

use	to	if you want to
The Open button 🖃 on the Standard toolbar, Open command on the File menu, or [Ctrl][O]	Open the Open dialog box	Open an existing file; a fast way to open a document when the New Document task pane is not displayed
The Documents or More Documents hyperlink in the New Document task pane	Open the Open dialog box	Open an existing file; a fast way to open a document when the New Document task pane is displayed
A filename hyperlink in the New Document task pane	Open the file in the document window	Open the file; a fast way to open a file that was recently opened on your computer
The Choose a document hyperlink in the New Document task pane	Open the New From Existing Document dialog box	Create a copy of an existing file; a fast way to open a document you intend to save with a new filename

FIGURE B-1: New Document task pane

Open button

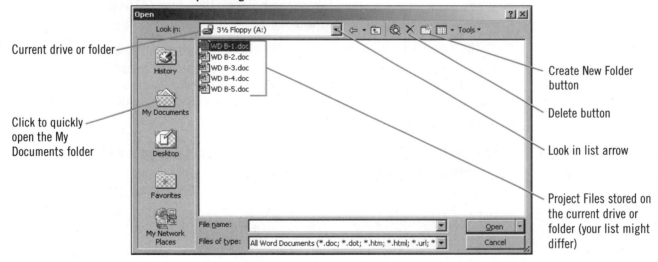

Your task pane might also include hyperlinks to recently opened files here

Documents hyperlink (yours might be the More Documents hyperlink)

Click to open an existing file as a new file

FIGURE B-2: Open dialog box

Current drive or folder

Click to quickly open the My Documents folder

Create New Folder button

Delete button

Look in list arrow

Project Files stored on the current drive or folder (your list might differ)

Managing files and folders

The Open and Save As dialog boxes include powerful tools for navigating, creating, and deleting files and folders on your computer, a network, or the Web. By selecting a file or folder and clicking the Delete button ⊠, you can delete the item and send it to the Recycle Bin. You can also create a new folder for storing files by clicking the Create New Folder button ⊡ and typing a name for the folder. The new folder is created in the current folder.

Using the Save As dialog box, you can also create new files that are based on existing files. You can create a new file by saving an existing file with a different filename or by saving it in a different location on your system. You also can save a file in a different file format so that it can be opened in a different software program. To save a file in a different format, click the Files of type list arrow, then click the type of file you want to create. For example, you can save a Word document (which has a .doc file extension) as a plain text file (.txt), as a Web page file (.htm), or in a variety of other file formats.

Selecting Text

Before deleting, editing, or formatting text, you must **select** the text. Selecting text involves clicking and dragging the I-beam pointer across text to highlight it. You also can click with the ✍ pointer in the blank area to the left of text to select lines or paragraphs. Table B-2 describes the many ways to select text. ⬛⬛⬛ Alice revises the press release by selecting text and replacing it with new text.

Steps

Trouble?

If you make a mistake, you can deselect the text by clicking anywhere in the document window.

1. **Click before December 9, 2002 and drag the I pointer over the text to select it**
   The date is selected, as shown in Figure B-3.

2. **Type January 13, 2003**
   The text you type replaces the selected text.

3. **Double-click James, type your first name, double-click Callaghan, then type your last name**
   Double-clicking a word selects the entire word.

4. **Place the pointer in the margin to the left of the phone number so that the pointer changes to ✍, click to select the phone number, then type (415) 555-8293**
   Clicking to the left of a line of text with the ✍ pointer selects the entire line.

5. **Click the down scroll arrow at the bottom of the vertical scroll bar until the headline Guy Fogg to Speak ... is at the top of your document window**
   The scroll arrows or scroll bars allow you to **scroll** through a document. You scroll through a document when you want to display different parts of the document in the document window.

6. **Select SAN FRANCISCO, then type NEW YORK**

QuickTip

If you delete text by mistake, immediately click the Undo button [⤺] on the Standard toolbar to restore the deleted text to the document.

7. **In the fourth body paragraph, select the sentence All events will be held at the St. James Hotel., then press [Delete]**
   Selecting text and pressing [Delete] removes the text from the document.

8. **Select and replace text in the second and last paragraphs using the following table:**

select	type
February 12	March 6
St. James Hotel in downtown San Francisco	Waldorf-Astoria Hotel
National Public Radio's Helen DeSaint	New York Times literary editor Isabel Eliot

   The edited press release is shown in Figure B-4.

9. **Click the Save button [💾] on the Standard toolbar**
   Your changes to the press release are saved. Always save before and after editing text.

CLUES TO USE

Replacing text in Overtype mode

Normally you must select text before typing to replace the existing characters, but by turning on **Overtype mode** you can type over existing characters without selecting them first. To turn Overtype mode on and off on your computer, double-click OVR in the status bar.

On some computers you also can turn Overtype mode on and off by pressing [Insert]. When Overtype mode is on, OVR appears in black in the status bar. When Overtype mode is off, OVR is dimmed.

FIGURE B-3: Date selected in the press release

Selected text

Left document margin

Down scroll arrow

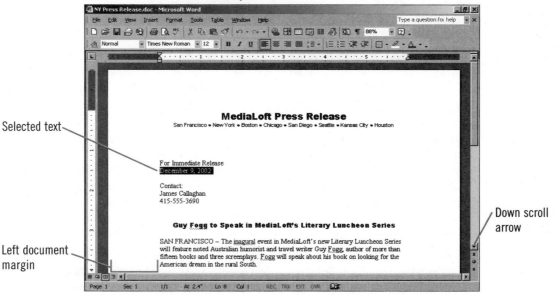

FIGURE B-4: Edited press release

Replacement text

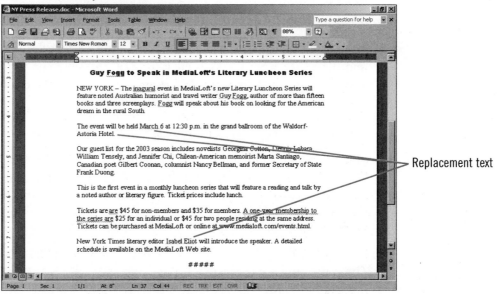

TABLE B-2: Methods for selecting text

to select	use the mouse pointer to
Any amount of text	Drag over the text
A word	Double-click the word
A line of text	Click with the ⤢ pointer to the left of the line
A sentence	Press and hold [Ctrl], then click the sentence
A paragraph	Triple-click the paragraph or double-click with the ⤢ pointer to the left of the paragraph
A large block of text	Click at the beginning of the selection, press and hold [Shift], then click at the end of the selection
Multiple nonconsecutive selections	Select the first selection, then press and hold [Ctrl] as you select each additional selection
An entire document	Triple-click with the ⤢ pointer to the left of any text, click Select All on the Edit menu, or press [Ctrl][A]

Cutting and Pasting Text

Word's editing features allow you to move text from one location to another in a document. The operation of moving text is often called **cut and paste.** When you cut text from a document, you remove it from the document and add it to the **Clipboard,** a temporary storage area for text and graphics that you cut or copy from a document. You cut text by selecting it and using the Cut button or the Cut command on the Edit menu. To insert the text from the Clipboard into the document, you place the insertion point where you want to insert the text, and then use the Paste button or the Paste command on the Edit menu to paste the text at that location. You also can move text by dragging it to a new location using the mouse. ✐ Alice reorganizes the information in the press release by moving text using the cut and paste and dragging methods.

Steps

1. Click the **Show/Hide ¶ button** ¶ on the Standard toolbar
   Formatting marks appear in the document window. **Formatting marks** are special characters that appear on your screen and do not print. Common formatting marks include the paragraph symbol (¶), which shows the end of a paragraph—wherever you press [Enter]; the dot symbol (·), which represents a space—wherever you press [Spacebar]; and the arrow symbol (→), which shows the location of a tab stop—wherever you press [Tab]. Working with formatting marks turned on can help you to select, edit, and format text with precision.

2. In the third paragraph, select **Canadian poet Gilbert Coonan,** (including the comma and the space after it), then click the **Cut button** ✂ on the Standard toolbar
   The text is removed from the document and placed on the Clipboard. Word uses two different clipboards: the **system Clipboard** (the Clipboard), which holds just one item, and the **Office Clipboard**, which holds up to 24 items. The last item you cut or copy is always added to both clipboards. You'll learn more about the Office Clipboard in a later lesson.

3. Place the insertion point before **novelists** (but after the space) in the first line of the third paragraph, then click the **Paste button** 📋 on the Standard toolbar
   The text is pasted at the location of the insertion point, as shown in Figure B-5. The Paste Options button 📋 appears below text when you first paste it in a document. You'll learn more about the Paste Options button in the next lesson. For now, you can ignore it.

4. Press **[Ctrl]**, then click the sentence **Ticket prices include lunch.** in the fourth paragraph
   The entire sentence is selected.

5. Press and hold the mouse button over the selected text until the pointer changes to ▷, then drag the pointer's vertical line to the end of the fifth paragraph (between the period and the paragraph mark) as shown in Figure B-6
   The pointer's vertical line indicates the location the text will be inserted when you release the mouse button.

6. Release the mouse button
   The selected text is moved to the location of the insertion point. It's convenient to move text using the dragging method when the locations of origin and destination are both visible on the screen. Text is not removed to the Clipboard when you move it using the dragging method.

7. Deselect the text, then click the **Save button** 💾 on the Standard toolbar
   Your changes to the press release are saved.

FIGURE B-5: Moved text with Paste Options button

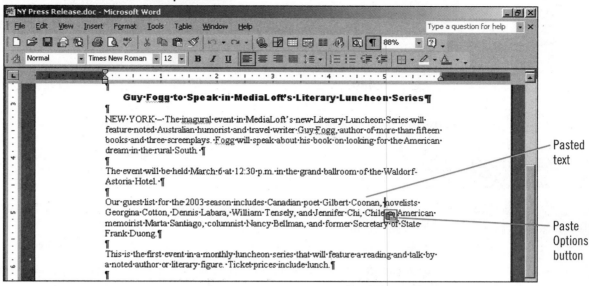

Pasted text

Paste Options button

FIGURE B-6: Text being dragged to a new location

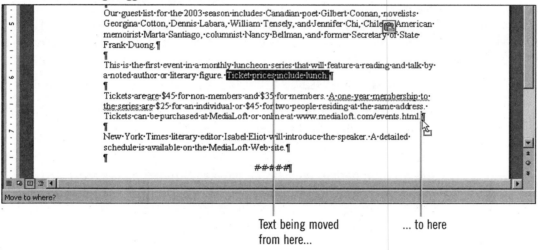

Text being moved from here...

... to here

Using keyboard shortcuts

Instead of using the Cut, Copy, and Paste commands to edit text in Word, you can use the keyboard shortcuts [Ctrl][X] to cut text, [Ctrl][C] to copy text, and [Ctrl][V] to paste text. A shortcut key is a function key, such as [F1], or a combination of keys, such as [Ctrl][S], that you press to perform a command. For example, pressing [Ctrl][S] saves changes to a document just as clicking the Save button or using the Save command on the File menu saves a document. Becoming skilled at using keyboard shortcuts can help you to quickly accomplish many of the tasks you perform frequently in Word. If a keyboard shortcut is available for a menu command, then it is listed next to the command on the menu. To find a more extensive list of shortcut keys, search the Help system using the keyword "shortcuts."

Copying and Pasting Text

Copying and pasting text is similar to cutting and pasting text, except that the text you copy is not removed from the document. Rather, a copy of the text is placed on the Clipboard, leaving the original text in place. You can copy text to the Clipboard by using the Copy command on the Edit menu or the Copy button, or you can copy text by pressing [Ctrl] as you drag the selected text from one location to another. ✐ Alice continues to edit the press release by copying text from one location to another.

Steps

Trouble?

If the Clipboard task pane opens, close it.

1. In the headline, select **Literary Luncheon**, then click the **Copy button** 📋 on the Standard toolbar

A copy of the text is placed on the Clipboard, leaving the text you copied in place.

2. Place the insertion point before **season** in the third body paragraph, then click the **Paste button** 📋 on the Standard toolbar

"Literary Luncheon" is inserted before "season," as shown in Figure B-7. Notice that the pasted text is formatted differently than the paragraph in which it was inserted.

QuickTip

If you don't like the result of a paste option, try another option or click the Undo button and then paste the text again.

3. Click the **Paste Options button** 📋▾, then click **Match Destination Formatting**

The Paste Options button allows you to change the formatting of pasted text. The formatting of "Literary Luncheon" is changed to match the rest of the paragraph. The options available on the Paste Options menu depend on the format of the text you are pasting and the format of the surrounding text. Table B-3 summarizes the commands used for pasting text.

4. Scroll down if necessary so that the last two paragraphs are visible on your screen

5. In the fifth paragraph, select **www.medialoft.com**, press and hold **[Ctrl]**, then press the mouse button until the pointer changes to 🔖

6. Drag the pointer's vertical line to the end of the last paragraph, placing it between **site** and the period, release the mouse button, then release [Ctrl]

The text is copied to the last paragraph. Since the formatting of the text you copied is the same as the formatting of the paragraph in which you inserted it, you can ignore the Paste Options button. Text is not copied to the Clipboard when you copy it using the dragging method.

7. Place the insertion point between **site** and **www.medialoft.com** in the last paragraph, type **at** followed by a space, then click the **Save button** 💾 on the Standard toolbar

Compare your document with Figure B-8.

CLUES TO USE

Using the Undo, Redo, and Repeat commands

Word remembers the editing and formatting changes you make so that you can easily reverse or repeat them. You can reverse the last action you took by clicking the Undo button ↶ on the Standard toolbar, or you can undo a series of actions by clicking the Undo list arrow ↶▾ and selecting the action you want to reverse. When you undo an action using the Undo list arrow, you also undo all the actions above it in the list; that is, all actions that were performed after the action you selected. Similarly, you can keep the changes you just reversed by using the Redo button ↷ and the Redo list arrow ↷▾.

If you want to repeat a change you just made, use the Repeat command on the Edit menu. The name of the Repeat command changes depending on the last action you took. For example, if you just typed "thank you," the name of the command will be Repeat Typing. Clicking the Repeat Typing command will insert "thank you" at the location of the insertion point. You also can repeat the last action you took by pressing [F4].

FIGURE B-7: Text pasted in document

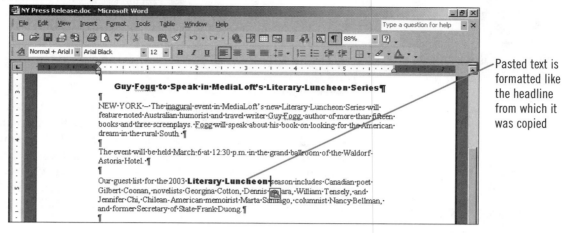

Pasted text is formatted like the headline from which it was copied

FIGURE B-8: Copied text in press release

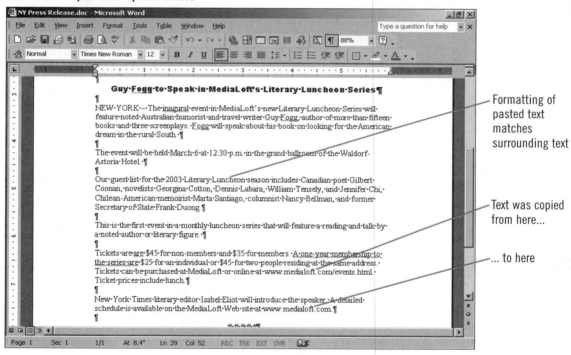

Formatting of pasted text matches surrounding text

Text was copied from here...

... to here

TABLE B-3: Commands used for pasting text

command	use to
Paste command on the Edit menu, Paste button 📋 **on the Standard toolbar, or [Ctrl][V]**	Insert the last item you cut or copied at the location of the insertion point; use the Paste Options button to change the format of the pasted text
Paste Special command on the Edit menu	Insert an item copied or cut from another Office program into a Word document; allows you to embed the object so that you can edit it in its original program; also allows you to create a link to the source file so that changes to the source file are reflected in the Word document
Paste as Hyperlink command on the Edit menu	Paste text so that it is formatted as a hyperlink that jumps to the location from where text was copied; can be used only in conjunction with the Copy command

Unit B

Word 2002

Using the Office Clipboard

The Office Clipboard allows you to collect text and graphics from files created in any Office Program and insert them into your Word documents. It holds up to 24 items and, unlike the system Clipboard, the items on the Office Clipboard can be viewed. By default, the Office Clipboard opens automatically when you cut or copy two items consecutively. You can also use the Office Clipboard command on the Edit menu to manually display the Office Clipboard if you prefer to work with it open. You add items to the Office Clipboard using the Cut and Copy commands. The last item you collect is always added to both the system Clipboard and the Office Clipboard. Alice uses the Office Clipboard to move several sentences in her press release.

Steps 1234

1. In the last paragraph, select the sentence **New York Times literary editor...** (including the space after the period), then click the **Cut button** ✂ on the Standard toolbar
   The sentence is cut to the Clipboard.

Trouble?

If the Office Clipboard does not open, click Office Clipboard on the Edit menu, click the Undo button on the Standard toolbar two times, click Clear All on the Clipboard task pane, then repeat steps 1 and 2. To restore the default, click Options on the Clipboard task pane, click Show Office Clipboard Automatically to select it, then click outside the menu.

2. Select the sentence **A detailed schedule is...** (including the ¶ mark), then click ✂
   The Office Clipboard opens in the Clipboard task pane, as shown in Figure B-9. It displays the items you cut from the press release. The 📄 icon next to each item indicates the items are from a Word document.

3. Place the insertion point at the end of the second paragraph (before the ¶ mark after Hotel.), then click the **New York Times literary editor...** item on the Office Clipboard
   Clicking an item on the Office Clipboard pastes the item in the document at the location of the insertion point. Notice that the item remains on the Office Clipboard even after you pasted it. Items remain on the Office Clipboard until you delete them or close all open Office programs. Also, if you add a 25th item to the Office Clipboard, the first item is deleted.

4. Place the insertion point at the end of the third paragraph (after Duong.), then click the **A detailed schedule is...** item on the Office Clipboard
   The sentence is pasted in the document.

QuickTip

To delete an individual item from the Office Clipboard, click the list arrow next to the item, then click Delete.

5. Select the fourth paragraph, which contains the sentence **This is the first event...** (including the ¶ mark), then click ✂
   The sentence is cut to the Office Clipboard. Notice that the last item collected displays at the top of the Clipboard task pane. The last item collected is also stored on the system Clipboard.

6. Place the insertion point at the beginning of the third paragraph (before Our...), click the **Paste button** 📋 on the Standard toolbar, then press **[Backspace]**
   The "This is the first ..." sentence is pasted at the beginning of the "Our guest list ..." paragraph. You can paste the last item collected using either the Paste command or the Office Clipboard.

7. Place the insertion point at the end of the third paragraph (before the ¶ mark), then press **[Delete]** twice
   The ¶ symbols and the blank line between the third and fourth paragraphs are deleted.

QuickTip

Many Word users prefer to work with formatting marks turned on at all times. Experiment for yourself and see which method you prefer.

8. Click the **Show/Hide ¶ button** ¶ on the Standard toolbar
   Compare your press release with Figure B-10.

9. Click the **Clear All button** on the Office Clipboard to remove the items from it, close the Clipboard task pane, press **[Ctrl][Home]**, then click the **Save button** 💾
   Pressing [Ctrl][Home] moves the insertion point to the top of the document.

FIGURE B-9: Office Clipboard in Clipboard task pane

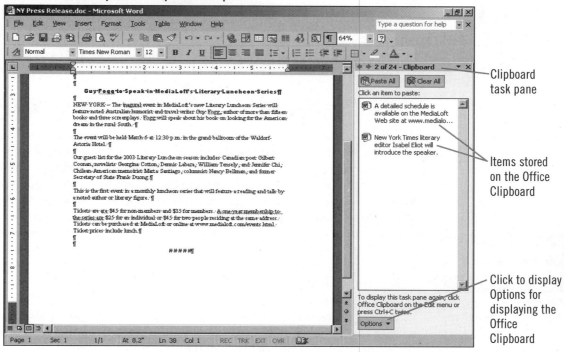

Clipboard task pane

Items stored on the Office Clipboard

Click to display Options for displaying the Office Clipboard

FIGURE B-10: Revised press release

Last item collected

Copying and moving items between documents

The system and Office Clipboards also can be used to copy and move items between Word documents. To copy or cut text from one Word document and paste it into another, first open both documents in the program window. When a document is open in the program window, a Word program button labeled with its filename appears on the taskbar. With multiple documents open, you can copy and move text between documents by copying or cutting the item(s) from one document and then switching to another document and pasting the item(s). To switch between open documents, click the button on the taskbar for the document you want to appear in the document window. The Office Clipboard stores all the items collected from all files, regardless of which document is displayed in the document window. The system Clipboard stores the last item collected from any file.

Using the Spelling and Grammar Checker and the Thesaurus

Word 2002

When you finish typing and revising a document, you can use the Spelling and Grammar command to search the document for misspelled words and grammatical errors. The Spelling and Grammar checker flags possible mistakes, suggests correct spellings, and offers remedies for grammatical errors such as subject-verb agreement, repeated words, and punctuation. Word also includes a Thesaurus, which you can use to look up synonyms for awkward or repetitive words. ✍ Alice uses the Spelling and Grammar checker to search her press release for errors. Before beginning the search, she sets the Spelling and Grammar checker to ignore words, such as Fogg, she knows are spelled correctly. She also uses the Thesaurus to find a synonym for "noted."

Trouble?

If Word flags your name or "MediaLoft" as misspelled, right-click those words, then click Ignore All.

1. **Right-click Fogg in the headline**
   A shortcut menu that includes suggestions for correcting the spelling of "Fogg"opens. You can correct individual spelling and grammar errors by right-clicking text that is underlined with a red or green wavy line and selecting a correction. Although "Fogg" is not in Word's dictionary, it is spelled correctly in the document.

2. **Click Ignore All**
   Clicking Ignore All tells Word not to flag "Fogg" as misspelled.

QuickTip

To change the language used by Word's proofing tools, click Tools on the menu bar, point to Language, then click Set Language.

3. **Press [Ctrl][Home], then click the Spelling and Grammar button** 🔤 **on the Standard toolbar**
   The Spelling and Grammar: English (U.S.) dialog box opens, as shown in Figure B-11. The dialog box identifies "inagural" as misspelled and suggests possible corrections for the error. The word selected in the Suggestions box is the correct spelling.

4. **Click Change**
   Word replaces the misspelled word with the correctly spelled word. Next, the dialog box indicates "are" is repeated in a sentence.

Trouble?

You might need to correct other spelling and grammatical errors.

5. **Click Delete**
   Word deletes the second occurrence of the repeated word. Next, the dialog box flags a subject-verb agreement error and suggests using "is" instead of "are," as shown in Figure B-12. The phrase selected in the Suggestions box is correct.

QuickTip

If Word does not offer a valid correction, correct the error yourself.

6. **Click Change**
   The word "is" replaces the word "are" in the sentence and the Spelling and Grammar dialog box closes. Keep in mind that the spelling and grammar feature identifies many common errors, but you cannot rely on it to find and correct all spelling and grammatical errors in your documents. Always proofread your documents carefully.

7. **Click OK to complete the spelling and grammar check, then scroll up until the headline is displayed at the top of your screen**

QuickTip

You also can right-click a word and point to Synonyms on the shortcut menu to see a list of synonyms for a word.

8. **In the first sentence of the third paragraph, select noted, click Tools on the menu bar, point to Language, then click Thesaurus**
   The Thesaurus: English (U.S.) dialog box opens, as shown in Figure B-13. Possible synonyms for "noted" appear in the dialog box.

9. **Click distinguished in the Replace with Synonym list box, then click Replace**
   The dialog box closes and "distinguished" replaces "noted" in the press release.

10. **Press [Ctrl][Home], then click the Save button** 💾 **on the Standard toolbar**

FIGURE B-11: **Spelling and Grammar: English (U.S.) dialog box**

Word identified as misspelled

Suggested corrections

Adds the misspelled word and the correction to the AutoCorrect list

Ignores this occurrence of the word

Leaves all occurrences of the word unchanged

Adds the word to Word's dictionary

Changes the word to the selected correction

Changes all occurrences of the word to the selected correction

FIGURE B-12: **Grammar error identified in Spelling and Grammar dialog box**

Grammar error identified

Possible corrections

Displays an explanation of the grammar rule applied to the error

FIGURE B-13: **Thesaurus: English (U.S.) dialog box**

Word in the document

Possible meanings for the word

Replaces the word with the selected synonym

Synonyms for the selected meaning of the word

Finding and Replacing Text

Word's Find and Replace feature allows you to automatically search for and replace all instances of a word or phrase in a document. For example, you might need to substitute "bookstore" for "store," and it would be very time-consuming to manually locate and replace each instance of "store" in a long document. Using the Replace command you can automatically find and replace all occurrences of specific text at once, or you can choose to find and review each occurrence individually. You also can use the Find command to locate and highlight every occurrence of a specific word or phrase in a document. ✒ MediaLoft has decided to change the name of the New York series from "Literary Luncheon Series" to "Literary Limelight Series." Alice uses the Replace command to search the document for all instances of "Luncheon" and replace them with "Limelight."

1. Click **Edit** on the menu bar, click **Replace**, then click **More** in the Find and Replace dialog box

   The Find and Replace dialog box opens, as shown in Figure B-14.

2. Click the **Find what text box**, then type **Luncheon**

   "Luncheon" is the text that will be replaced.

3. Press **[Tab]**, then type **Limelight** in the Replace with text box

   "Limelight" is the text that will replace "Luncheon."

4. Click the **Match case check box** in the Search Options section to select it

   Selecting the Match case check box tells Word to find only exact matches for the uppercase and lowercase characters you entered in the Find what text box. You want to replace all instances of "Luncheon" in the proper name "Literary Luncheon Series." You do not want to replace "luncheon" when it refers to a lunchtime event.

QuickTip

Click Find Next to find, review, and replace each occurrence individually.

5. Click **Replace All**

   Clicking Replace All changes all occurrences of "Luncheon" to "Limelight" in the press release. A message box reports three replacements were made.

6. Click **OK** to close the message box, then click **Close** to close the Find and Replace dialog box

   Word replaced "Luncheon" with "Limelight" in three locations, but did not replace "luncheon."

7. Click **Edit** on the menu bar, then click **Find**

   The Find and Replace dialog box opens with the Find tab displayed. The Find command allows you to quickly locate all instances of text in a document. You can use it to verify that Word did not replace "luncheon."

8. Type **luncheon** in the Find what text box, click the **Highlight all items found in check box** to select it, click **Find All**, then click **Close**

   The Find and Replace dialog box closes and "luncheon" is selected in the document.

9. Deselect the text, click the **Save button** 🖫 on the Standard toolbar, then click the **Print button** 🖨 on the Standard toolbar

   A copy of the finished press release prints. Compare your document to Figure B-15.

10. Click **File** on the menu bar, then click **Close**

Replace only exact matches of uppercase and lowercase characters

Find only complete words

Use wildcards (*) in a search string

Find words that sound like the Find what text

Find and replace all forms of a word

FIGURE B-15: Completed press release

MediaLoft Press Release

San Francisco • New York • Boston • Chicago • San Diego • Seattle • Kansas City • Houston

For Immediate Release
January 13, 2003

Contact:
Alice Wegman
(415) 555-8293

Guy Fogg to Speak in MediaLoft's Literary Limelight Series

NEW YORK – The inaugural event in MediaLoft's new Literary Limelight Series will feature noted Australian humorist and travel writer Guy Fogg, author of more than fifteen books and three screenplays. Fogg will speak about his book on looking for the American dream in the rural South.

The event will be held March 6 at 12:30 p.m. in the grand ballroom of the Waldorf-Astoria Hotel. New York Times literary editor Isabel Eliot will introduce the speaker.

This is the first event in a monthly luncheon series that will feature a reading and talk by a distinguished author or literary figure. Our guest list for the 2003 Literary Limelight season includes Canadian poet Gilbert Coonan, novelists Georgina Cotton, Dennis Labara, William Tensely, and Jennifer Chi, Chilean-American memoirist Marta Santiago, columnist Nancy Bellman, and former Secretary of State Frank Duong. A detailed schedule is available on the MediaLoft Web site at www.medialoft.com.

Tickets are $45 for non-members and $35 for members. A one-year membership to the series is $25 for an individual or $45 for two people residing at the same address. Tickets can be purchased at MediaLoft or online at www.medialoft.com/events.html. Ticket prices include lunch.

#

CLUES TO USE

Inserting text with AutoCorrect

As you type, AutoCorrect automatically corrects many commonly misspelled words. By creating your own AutoCorrect entries, you also can set Word to quickly insert text that you type often, such as your name or contact information, or to correct words you frequently misspell. For example, you could create an AutoCorrect entry so that "Alice Wegman" is automatically inserted whenever you type "aw" followed by a space. To create an AutoCorrect entry, click AutoCorrect Options on the Tools menu. On the AutoCorrect tab in the AutoCorrect dialog box, type the text you want to be automatically corrected in the Replace text box (such as "aw"), type the text you want to be automatically inserted in its place in the With text box (such as "Alice Wegman"), then click Add. The AutoCorrect entry is added to the list. Note that Word inserts an AutoCorrect entry in a document only when you press [Spacebar] after typing the text you want Word to correct. For example, Word will insert "Alice Wegman" when you type "aw" followed by a space, but not when you type "awful."

Using Wizards and Templates

Word includes many templates that you can use to quickly create memos, faxes, letters, reports, brochures, and other professionally designed documents. A **template** is a formatted document that contains placeholder text. To create a document that is based on a template, you replace the placeholder text with your own text and then save the document with a new filename. A **wizard** is an interactive set of dialog boxes that guides you through the process of creating a document. A wizard prompts you to provide information and select formatting options, and then it creates the document for you based on your specifications. You can create a document with a wizard or template using the New command on the File menu. ✎ Alice will fax the press release to her list of press contacts, beginning with the *New York Times*. She uses a template to create a fax coversheet for the press release.

1. Click **File** on the menu bar, then click **New**
   The New Document task pane opens.

2. Click the **General Templates hyperlink** in the New Document task pane
   The Templates dialog box opens. The tabs in the dialog box contain icons for the Word templates and wizards.

3. Click the **Letters & Faxes tab**, then click the **Professional Fax** icon
   A preview of the Professional Fax template appears in the Templates dialog box, as shown in Figure B-16.

> **QuickTip**
> Double-clicking an icon in the Templates dialog box also opens a new document based on the template.

4. Click **OK**
   The Professional Fax template opens as a new document in the document window. It contains placeholder text, which you can replace with your own information.

5. Drag to select **Company Name Here**, then type **MediaLoft**

6. Click the **Click here and type return address and phone and fax numbers placeholder**
   Clicking the placeholder selects it. When a placeholder says Click here… you do not need to drag to select it.

7. Type **MediaLoft San Francisco**, press **[Enter]**, then type **Tel: (415) 555-8293**
   The text you type replaces the placeholder text.

> **QuickTip**
> Delete any placeholder text you do not want to replace.

8. Replace the remaining placeholder text with the text shown in Figure B-17
   Word automatically inserted the current date in the document. You do not need to replace the current date with the date shown in the figure.

9. Click **File** on the menu bar, click **Save As**, use the Save in list arrow to navigate to the drive or folder where your Project Files are located, type **NYT Fax** in the File name text box, then click **Save**
   The document is saved with the filename NYT Fax.

10. Click the **Print button** 🖨 on the Standard toolbar, click **File** on the menu bar, then click **Exit**
    A copy of the fax coversheet prints and the document and Word close.

FIGURE B-16: Letters & Faxes tab in Templates dialog box

Preview of selected template

FIGURE B-17: Completed fax coversheet document

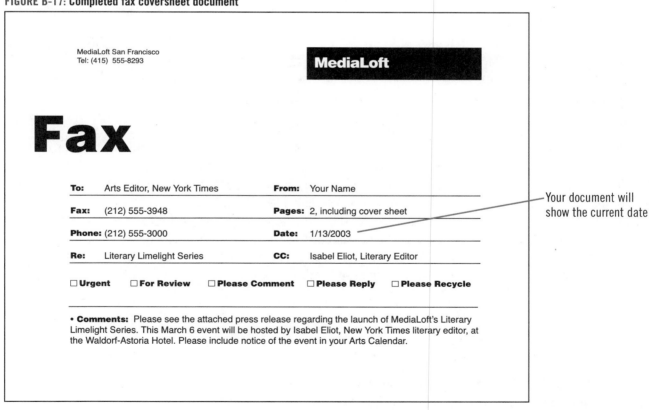

Your document will show the current date

Word 2002

Practice

► Concepts Review

Label the elements of the Open dialog box shown in Figure B-18.

FIGURE B-18

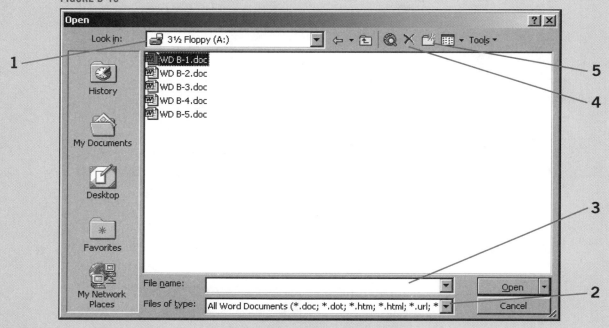

Match each term with the statement that best describes it.

6. **System Clipboard**
7. **Show/Hide**
8. **Select**
9. **Thesaurus**
10. **Undo**
11. **Template**
12. **Office Clipboard**
13. **Paste**
14. **Replace**

a. Feature used to suggest synonyms for words
b. Command used to insert text stored on the Clipboard into a document
c. Command used to reverse the last action you took in a document
d. Temporary storage area for only the last item cut or copied from a document
e. Document that contains placeholder text
f. Temporary storage area for up to 24 items collected from any Office file
g. Command used to locate and replace occurrences of specific text in a document
h. Action that must be taken before text can be cut, copied, or deleted
i. Command used to display formatting marks in a document

Select the best answer from the list of choices.

15. **Which of the following is *not* used to open an existing document?**
    a. Documents or More documents hyperlink in the New Document task pane
    b. Open command on the Edit menu
    c. Blank document hyperlink in the New Document task pane
    d. Open button on the Standard toolbar

16. To locate and change all instances of a word in a document, which command do you use?
- **a.** Replace
- **b.** Find
- **c.** Search
- **d.** Paste

17. Which of the following statements is _not_ true?
- **a.** The last item cut or copied from a document is stored on the system Clipboard.
- **b.** The Office Clipboard can hold more than one item.
- **c.** You can view the contents of the Office Clipboard.
- **d.** When you move text by dragging it, a copy of the text you move is stored on the system Clipboard.

18. Which Word feature corrects errors as you type?
- **a.** AutoCorrect
- **b.** Thesaurus
- **c.** Spelling and Grammar
- **d.** Undo and Redo

19. Which command do you use to paste an item created in a different Office program into a Word document so that changes to the source file are reflected in the Word document?
- **a.** Paste
- **b.** Paste Special
- **c.** Paste as Hyperlink
- **d.** Office Clipboard

20. What does the symbol ¶ represent when it is displayed in the document window?
- **a.** Text that is pasted
- **b.** A space
- **c.** The end of a paragraph
- **d.** A tab stop

► Skills Review

1. Open a document.
- **a.** Start Word, click the Open button, then open the file WD B-2 from the drive and folder where your Project Files are located.
- **b.** Save the document with the filename **CAOS Press Release**.

2. Select text.
- **a.** Select **Today's Date** and replace it with the current date.
- **b.** Select **Your Name** and **Your Phone Number** and replace them with the relevant information.
- **c.** Scroll down, then select and replace text in the body of the press release using the following table as a guide:

in paragraph	select	replace with
1	16 and 17	13 and 14
1	fifth	eighth
4	open his renovated Pearl St studio for the first time this year	offer a sneak-preview of his Peace sculpture commissioned by the city of Prague

- **d.** In the fourth paragraph, delete the sentence **Exhibiting with him will be sculptor Francis Pilo**.
- **e.** Save your changes to the press release.

3. Cut and paste text.

a. Display paragraph and other formatting marks in your document if they are not already displayed.

b. Use the Cut and Paste buttons to switch the order of the two sentences in the fourth paragraph (which begins New group shows...).

c. Use the drag method to switch the order of the second and third paragraphs.

d. Adjust the spacing if necessary so that there is one blank line between paragraphs, then save your changes.

4. Copy and paste text.

a. Use the Copy and Paste buttons to copy **CAOS 2000** from the headline and paste it before the word **map** in the third paragraph.

b. Change the formatting of the pasted text to match the formatting of the third paragraph, then insert a space between **2000** and **map** if necessary.

c. Use the drag method to copy **CAOS** from the third paragraph and paste it before the word **group** in the second sentence of the fourth paragraph, then save your changes.

5. Use the Office Clipboard.

a. Use the Office Clipboard command on the Edit menu to open the Office Clipboard in the task pane.

b. Scroll so that the first body paragraph is displayed at the top of the document window.

c. Select the **fifth paragraph** (which begins Studio location maps...) and cut it to the Office Clipboard.

d. Select the **third paragraph** (which begins Cambridgeport is easily accessible...) and cut it to the Office Clipboard.

e. Use the Office Clipboard to paste the Studio location maps... item as the new fourth paragraph.

f. Use the Office Clipboard to paste the Cambridgeport is easily accessible... item as the new fifth paragraph.

g. Use any method to switch the order of the two sentences in the fourth paragraph (which begins Studio location maps...).

h. Adjust the spacing if necessary so that there is one blank line between each of the six body paragraphs.

i. Turn off the display of formatting marks, clear and close the Office Clipboard, then save your changes.

6. Use the Spelling and Grammar checker and the Thesaurus.

a. Set Word to ignore the spelling of Cambridgeport, if necessary. (*Hint*: Right-click Cambridgeport.)

b. Move the insertion point to the top of the document, then use the Spelling and Grammar command to search for and correct any spelling and grammatical errors in the press release.

c. Use the Thesaurus to replace **thriving** in the second paragraph with a different suitable word.

d. Save your changes to the press release.

7. Find and replace text.

a. Using the Replace command, replace all instances of **2000** with **2003**.

b. Replace all instances of the abbreviation **St** with **Street**, taking care to replace whole words only when you perform the replace. (*Hint*: Click More to expand the Find and Replace dialog box.)

c. Use the Find command to find all instances of **st** in the document, and make sure no errors occurred when you replaced St with Street.

d. Proofread your press release, correct any errors, save your changes, print a copy, then close the document.

8. Use wizards and templates.

a. Use the New command to open the New Documents task pane.

b. Use the General Templates hyperlink to open the Templates dialog box.

c. Create a new document using the Elegant Fax template.

d. Replace the placeholder text in the document using Figure B-19 as a guide. Delete any placeholders that do not apply to your fax. The date in your fax will be the current date.

e. Scroll to the bottom of the document and replace the placeholder text with your return address.

f. Save the document as **CAOS Fax**, print a copy, close the document, then exit Word.

FIGURE B-19

CAOS 2003

FACSIMILE TRANSMITTAL SHEET

TO:	FROM:
Pat Zabko, Listings Editor	Your Name
COMPANY:	DATE:
Boston Phoenix	9/12/2003
FAX NUMBER :	TOTAL NO. OF PAGES INCLUDING COVER:
(617) 555-2980	2
PHONE NUMBER:	SENDER'S REFERENCE NUMBER:
RE:	YOUR REFERENCE NUMBER:
Cambridgeport Artists Open Studios	

☐URGENT ☐FOR REVIEW ☐PLEASE COMMENT ☐PLEASE REPLY ☐PLEASE RECYCLE

NOTES/COMMENTS:

A press release regarding the 2003 Cambridgeport Artists Open Studios is included with this fax. Please include this information in the Phoenix Listings.

▶ Independent Challenge 1

Because of your success in revitalizing a historic theatre in Hobart, Tasmania, you were hired as the director of The Wellington Lyric Theatre in Wellington, New Zealand, to breathe life into its theatre revitalization efforts. After a year on the job, you are launching your first major fund-raising drive. You'll create a fund-raising letter for the Lyric Theatre by modifying a letter you wrote for the theatre in Hobart.

a. Start Word, open the file WD B-3 from the drive and folder where your Project Files are located, then save it as **Lyric Theatre Letter**.

b. Replace the theatre name and address, the date, the inside address, and the salutation with the text shown in Figure B-20.

c. Use the Replace command to replace all instances of **Hobart** with **Wellington**.

d. Use the Replace command to replace all instances of **Tasmanians** with **New Zealanders**.

e. Use the Find command to locate the word **considerable**, then use the Thesaurus to replace the word with a synonym.

f. Create an AutoCorrect entry that inserts **Wellington Lyric Theatre** whenever you type **wlt**.

g. Select each XXXXX and the space that follows it, then type **wlt** followed by a space.

h. Move the fourth body paragraph so that it becomes the second body paragraph.

FIGURE B-20

The Wellington Lyric Theatre
72-74 Hobson Street, Thorndon, Wellington, New Zealand

September 12, 2003

Mr. Colin Fuller
168 Cuba Street
Wellington

Dear Mr. Fuller,

i. Replace Your Name with your name in the signature block.

j. Use the Spelling and Grammar command to check for and correct spelling and grammar errors.

k. Proofread the letter, correct any errors, save your changes, print a copy, close the document, then exit Word.

► Independent Challenge 2

An advertisement for job openings in Scotland caught your eye and you have decided to apply. The ad, shown in Figure B-21, was printed in last weekend's edition of your local newspaper. You'll use the Letter Wizard to create a cover letter to send with your resume.

a. Read the ad shown in Figure B-21 and decide which position to apply for. Choose the position that most closely matches your qualifications.

b. Start Word and open the Templates dialog box.

c. Double-click Letter Wizard on the Letters & Faxes tab, then select Send one letter in the Office Assistant balloon or Letter Wizard dialog box.

d. In the Letter Wizard—Step 1 of 4 dialog box, choose to include a date on your letter, select Elegant Letter for the page design, select Modified block for the letter style, include a header and footer with the page design, then click Next.

e. In the Letter Wizard—Step 2 of 4 dialog box, enter the recipient's name (Ms. Hillary Price) and the delivery address, referring to the ad for the address information. Also enter the salutation **Dear Ms. Price** using the business style, then click Next.

f. In the Letter Wizard—Step 3 of 4 dialog box, include a reference line in the letter, enter the appropriate position code (see Figure B-21) in the Reference line text box, then click Next.

g. In the Letter Wizard—Step 4 of 4 dialog box, enter your name as the sender, enter your return address (including your country), and select an appropriate complimentary closing. Then, because you will be including your resume with the letter, include one enclosure. Click Finish when you are done.

h. Click Cancel to close the Office Assistant, if necessary. Then save the letter with the filename **Global Dynamics Letter** to the drive and folder where your Project Files are located.

i. Replace the placeholder text in the body of the letter with three paragraphs that address your qualifications for the job:
   • In the first paragraph, specify the job you are applying for, indicate where you saw the position advertised, and briefly state your qualifications and interest in the position.

FIGURE B-21

*Global*Dynamics

Career Opportunities in Scotland

Global Dynamics, an established software development firm with offices in North America, Asia, and Europe, is seeking candidates for the following positions in its new Edinburgh facility:

Instructor

Responsible for delivering software training to our expanding European customer base. Duties include delivering hands-on training, keeping up-to-date with product development, and working with the Director of Training to ensure the high quality of course materials. Successful candidate will have excellent presentation skills and be proficient in Microsoft PowerPoint and Microsoft Word. **Position B12C6**

Administrative Assistant

Proficiency with Microsoft Word a must! Administrative office duties include making travel arrangements, scheduling meetings, taking notes and publishing meeting minutes, handling correspondence, and ordering office supplies. Must have superb multi-tasking abilities, excellent communication, organizational, and interpersonal skills, and be comfortable working with e-mail and the Internet. **Position B16F5**

Copywriter

The ideal candidate will have marketing or advertising writing experience in a high tech environment, including collateral, newsletters, and direct mail. Experience writing for the Web, broadcast, and multimedia is a plus. Fluency with Microsoft Word required. **Position C13D4**

Positions offer salary, excellent benefits, moving expenses, and career growth opportunities.

Send resume and cover letter referencing position code to:

**Hillary Price
Director of Recruiting
Global Dynamics
24 Castle Terrace
Edinburgh EH3 9SH
United Kingdom**

- In the second paragraph, describe your work experience and skills. Be sure to relate your experience and qualifications to the position requirements listed in the ad.
- In the third paragraph, politely request an interview for the position and provide your phone number and e-mail address.

j. When you are finished typing the letter, check it for spelling and grammar errors and correct any mistakes.

k. Save your changes to the letter, print a copy, close the document, then exit Word.

▶ Independent Challenge 3

As administrative director of continuing education, you drafted a memo to instructors asking them to help you finalize the course schedule for next semester. Today you'll examine the draft and make revisions before printing it.

a. Start Word and open the file WD B-4 from the drive and folder where your Project Files are located.

b. Open the Save As dialog box, navigate to the drive and folder where your Project Files are located, use the Create New Folder button to create a new folder called **Memos**, then save the document as **Computer Memo** in the Memos folder.

c. Replace Your Name with your name in the From line.

d. Use the Cut and Paste buttons to move the sentence **If you are planning to teach ...** from the first body paragraph to become the first sentence in the last paragraph of the memo.

e. Use the [Delete] key to merge the first two paragraphs into one paragraph.

f. Use the Office Clipboard to reorganize the list of twelve-week courses so that the courses are listed in alphabetical order. (*Hint*: Use the Zoom list arrow to enlarge the document as needed.)

g. Use the dragging method to reorganize the list of one-day seminars so that the seminars are listed in alphabetical order.

h. Use the Spelling and Grammar command to check for and correct spelling and grammar errors.

i. Clear and close the Office Clipboard, save your changes, print a copy, close the document, then exit Word.

Independent Challenge 4

Reference sources—dictionaries, thesauri, style and grammar guides, and guides to business etiquette and procedure—are essential for day-to-day use in the workplace. Much of this reference information is available on the World Wide Web. In this independent challenge, you will locate reference sources on the Web and use some of them to look up definitions, synonyms, and antonyms for words. Your goal is to familiarize yourself with online reference sources so you can use them later in your work.

a. Start Word, open the file WD B-5 from the drive and folder where your Project Files are located, and save it as **Web References**. This document contains the questions you will answer about the Web reference sources you find. You will type your answers to the questions in the document.

b. Replace the placeholder text at the top of the Web References document with your name and the date.

c. Use your favorite search engine to search the Web for grammar and style guides, dictionaries, and thesauri. Use the keywords **grammar**, **usage**, **dictionary**, **glossary**, and **thesaurus** to conduct your search. If your search does not result in links to appropriate reference sources, try the following Web sites: www.bartleby.com, www.dictionary.com, or www.thesaurus.com.

d. Complete the Web References document, then proofread it and correct any mistakes.

e. Save the document, print a copy, close the document, then exit Word.

► Visual Workshop

Using the Contemporary Letter template, create the letter shown in Figure B-22. Save the document as **Visa Letter**.
Check the letter for spelling and grammar errors, then print a copy.

FIGURE B-22

35 Hardy Street
Vancouver, BC V6C 3K4
Tel: (604) 555-8989
Fax: (604) 555-8981

Your Name

March 10, 2003

Embassy of Australia
Suite 710
50 O'Connor Street
Ottawa, Ontario K1P 6L2

Dear Sir or Madam:

I am applying for a long-stay (six-month) tourist visa to Australia, valid for four years. I am
scheduled to depart for Sydney on June 1, 2003, returning to Vancouver on November 23, 2003.

While in Australia, I plan to conduct research for a book I am writing on coral reefs. I am interested
in a multiple entry visa valid for four years so that I can return to Australia after this trip to follow-up
on my initial research. I will be based in Cairns, but will be traveling frequently to other parts of
Australia to meet with scientists, policy-makers, and environmentalists.

Enclosed please find my completed visa application form, my passport, a passport photo, a copy of
my return air ticket, and the visa fee. Please let me know if I can provide further information.

Sincerely,

Your Name

Enclosures (5)

Formatting

Text and Paragraphs

Objectives

- MOUS ▶ **Format with fonts**
- MOUS ▶ **Change font styles and effects**
- MOUS ▶ **Change line and paragraph spacing**
- MOUS ▶ **Align paragraphs**
- MOUS ▶ **Work with tabs**
- MOUS ▶ **Work with indents**
- MOUS ▶ **Add bullets and numbering**
- MOUS ▶ **Add borders and shading**

Formatting can enhance the appearance of a document, create visual impact, and help illustrate a document's structure. The formatting of a document can also add personality and lend a degree of professionalism to your document. In this unit you learn how to format text using different fonts and font-formatting options. You also learn how to change the alignment, indentation, and spacing of paragraphs, and how to spruce up documents with borders, shading, bullets, and other paragraph-formatting effects. Isaac Robinson is the marketing director at the MediaLoft Chicago store. Isaac has drafted a quarterly marketing report to send to MediaLoft's headquarters. He now needs to format the report so it is attractive and highlights the significant information. You will work with Isaac as he formats the report.

Formatting with Fonts

Formatting text with different fonts is a quick and powerful way to enhance the appearance of a document. A **font** is a complete set of characters with the same typeface or design. Arial, Times New Roman, Comic Sans, Courier, and Tahoma are some of the more common fonts, but there are hundreds of others, each with a specific design and feel. Another way to alter the impact of text is to increase or decrease its **font size**, which is measured in points. A **point** is ½ of an inch. When formatting a document with fonts, it's important to pick fonts that augment the document's purpose. You can apply fonts and font sizes to text by selecting the text and using the Formatting toolbar. ✐ Isaac changes the font and font size of the title and headings in his report, selecting a font that enhances the business tone of the document. By formatting the title and headings in a font different from the body text, he helps to visually structure the report for readers.

Steps 1 2 3 4

1. Start **Word**, open the file **WD C-1** from the drive and folder where your Project Files are located, then save it as **Chicago Marketing Report**
   The file opens in Print Layout view.

2. Click the **Normal View button** 🔲 on the horizontal scroll bar, click the **Zoom list arrow** on the Standard toolbar, then click **100%** if necessary
   The document switches to Normal view, a view useful for simple text formatting. The name of the font used in the document, Times New Roman, is displayed in the Font list box on the Formatting toolbar. The font size, 12, appears next to it in the Font Size list box.

3. Select the title **MediaLoft Chicago Quarterly Marketing Report**, then click the **Font list arrow** on the Formatting toolbar
   The Font list showing the fonts available on your computer opens, as shown in Figure C-1. Fonts you have used recently appear above the double line. All the fonts on your computer are listed in alphabetical order below the double line.

4. Click **Arial**
   The font of the report title changes to Arial.

5. Click the **Font Size list arrow** on the Formatting toolbar, then click **20**
   The font size of the title increases to 20 points.

6. Click the **Font Color list arrow** 🄰▾ on the Formatting toolbar
   A palette of colors opens.

7. Click **Dark Blue** on the Font Color palette as shown in Figure C-2, then deselect the text
   The color of the report title text changes to dark blue. The active color on the Font Color button also changes to dark blue.

8. Select the heading **Advertising**, click the **Font list arrow**, click **Arial**, click the **Font Size list arrow**, click **14**, click the **Font Color button** 🄰, then deselect the text
   The heading is formatted in 14-point Arial with a dark blue color.

9. Scroll down the document and format each of the following headings in 14-point Arial with a dark blue color: **Events**, **Classes & Workshops**, **Publications**, and **Surveys**

10. Press **[Ctrl][Home]**, then click the **Save button** 🔲 on the Standard toolbar
    Pressing [Ctrl][Home] moves the insertion point to the beginning of the document. Compare your document to Figure C-3.

FIGURE C-1: Font list

FIGURE C-1: Font list

Font list arrow

Font Size list arrow

Font names are formatted in the font itself (your list might differ)

FIGURE C-2: Font Color palette

Font Color list arrow

Name of color appears as a ScreenTip

Click to create a custom color

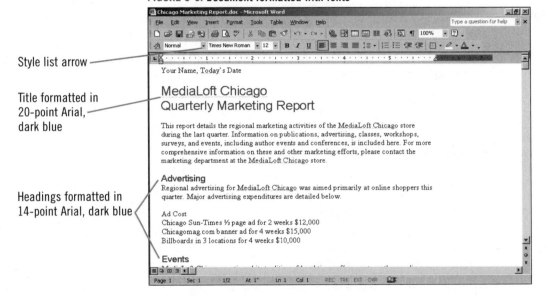

FIGURE C-3: Document formatted with fonts

Style list arrow

Title formatted in 20-point Arial, dark blue

Headings formatted in 14-point Arial, dark blue

Clearing text formatting

If you are unhappy with the way text is formatted, you can use the Clear Formats command to return the text to the default format settings. By default, text is formatted in 12-point Times New Roman and paragraphs are left-aligned and single-spaced. To clear formatting from text, select the text you want to clear, point to Clear on the Edit menu, then click Formats. Alternately, click the Styles list arrow on the Formatting toolbar, then click Clear Formatting. Clearing formatting from text does not delete or change the text itself; it simply formats the text with the default format settings.

Changing Font Styles and Effects

You can dramatically change the appearance of text by applying different font styles, font effects, and character-spacing effects. For example, you can use the buttons on the Formatting toolbar to make text darker by applying **bold**, or to slant text by applying *italic*. You can also use the Font command on the Format menu to apply font effects and character-spacing effects to text. Isaac spices up the appearance of the text in his document by applying different font styles and effects.

Steps

QuickTip

Click the Underline button ⓤ on the Formatting toolbar to underline text.

1. Select **MediaLoft Chicago Quarterly Marketing Report**, then click the **Bold button** Ⓑ on the Formatting toolbar

   Applying bold makes the characters darker and thicker.

2. Select the **paragraph** under the title, then click the **Italic button** Ⓘ on the Formatting toolbar

   The paragraph is formatted in italic.

QuickTip

To quickly apply bold to multiple headings, press and hold [Ctrl] as you select each heading, then click Ⓑ.

3. Scroll down and apply bold to each dark blue heading

   The headings all have a darker, thicker appearance.

4. Scroll up until the subheading Author Events is at the top of your screen, select **Author Events**, click **Format** on the menu bar, then click **Font**

   The Font dialog box opens, as shown in Figure C-4. You can use the Font tab to change the font, font style, size, and color of text, and to add an underline and apply font effects to the selected text.

5. Scroll up the Font list, click **Arial**, click **Bold Italic** in the Font style list box, select the **Small caps check box**, then click **OK**

   The subheading is formatted in Arial, bold, italic, and small caps. When you change text to small caps, the lowercase letters are changed to uppercase letters in a smaller font size.

QuickTip

If you apply formats one by one, then pressing [F4] repeats only the last format you applied.

6. Select **Travel Writers & Photographers Conference**, then press **[F4]**

   Pressing [F4] repeats the last action you took. Because you last applied Arial, bold, italic, and small caps together in one action (using the Font dialog box), the subheading is formatted in Arial, bold, italic, and small caps.

7. Under Author Events, select the book title **Just H20 Please: Tales of True Adventure on the Environmental Frontline**, click Ⓘ, select **2** in the book title, click **Format** on the menu bar, click **Font**, click the **Subscript check box**, click **OK**, then deselect the text

   As shown in Figure C-5, the book title is formatted in italic and the character 2 is subscript.

QuickTip

To animate the selected text, click the Text Effects tab in the Font dialog box, then select an animation style. The animation appears only when a document is viewed in Word; animation effects do not print.

8. Press **[Ctrl][Home]**, select the **report title**, click **Format** on the menu bar, click **Font**, then click the **Character Spacing tab** in the Font dialog box

   You use the Character Spacing tab to change the scale, or width, of the selected characters, to alter the spacing between characters, or to raise or lower the position of the characters.

9. Click the **Scale list arrow**, click **150%**, click **OK**, deselect the text, then click the **Save button** 🖫 on the Standard toolbar

   Increasing the scale of the characters makes them wider and gives the text a shorter, squat appearance, as shown in Figure C-6.

FIGURE C-4: Font tab in Font dialog box

Shows the combined results of the selected formats

Select font, font style, and font size

Select font color and underline style

Select font effects

FIGURE C-5: Font effects applied to text

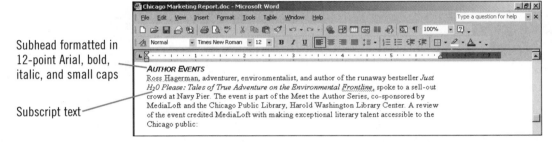

Subhead formatted in 12-point Arial, bold, italic, and small caps

Subscript text

FIGURE C-6: Character-spacing effects applied to text

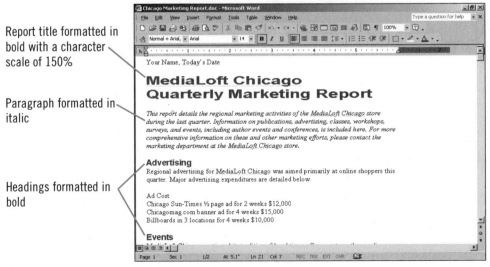

Report title formatted in bold with a character scale of 150%

Paragraph formatted in italic

Headings formatted in bold

CLUES TO USE

Changing the case of letters

The Change Case command on the Format menu allows you to quickly change letters from uppercase to lowercase—and vice versa—saving you the time it takes to retype text you want to change. To change the case of selected text, use the Change Case command to open the Change Case dialog box, then select the case style you want to use. Sentence case capitalizes the first letter of a sentence, title case capitalizes the first letter of each word, and toggle case switches all letters to the opposite case.

Word 2002

Changing Line and Paragraph Spacing

Increasing the amount of space between lines adds more white space to a document and can make it easier to read. Adding space between paragraphs can also open up a document and improve its appearance. You can change line and paragraph spacing using the Paragraph command on the Format menu. You can also use the Line Spacing button to quickly change line spacing. ✎ Isaac increases the line spacing of several paragraphs and adds extra space under each heading to give the report a more open feel.

Steps 1 2 3 4

QuickTip

The checkmark on the Line Spacing list indicates the current line spacing.

1. Place the insertion point in the italicized paragraph under the report title, then click the **Line Spacing list arrow** 📋▾ on the Formatting toolbar
   The Line Spacing list opens. This list includes options for increasing the space between lines.

2. Click **1.5**
   The space between the lines in the paragraph increases to 1.5 lines. Notice that you do not need to select an entire paragraph to change its paragraph formatting; simply place the insertion point in the paragraph you want to format.

QuickTip

Word recognizes any string of text that ends with a paragraph mark as a paragraph, including titles, headings, and single lines in a list.

3. Scroll down until the heading Advertising is at the top of your screen, select the **four-line list** that begins with Ad Cost, click 📋▾, then click **1.5**
   The line spacing between the selected paragraphs changes to 1.5. To change the paragraph-formatting features of more than one paragraph, you must select the paragraphs.

4. Place the insertion point in the heading **Advertising**, click **Format** on the menu bar, then click **Paragraph**
   The Paragraph dialog box opens, as shown in Figure C-7. You can use the Indents and Spacing tab to change line spacing and the spacing above and below paragraphs. Spacing between paragraphs is measured in points.

QuickTip

Adjusting the space between paragraphs is a more precise way to add white space to a document than inserting blank lines.

5. Click the **After up arrow** in the Spacing section so that 6 pt appears, then click **OK**
   Six points of space are added below the paragraph—the Advertising heading.

6. Select **Advertising**, then click the **Format Painter button** 🖌 on the Standard toolbar
   The pointer changes to 🖌I. The **Format Painter** is a powerful Word feature that allows you to copy all the format settings applied to the selected text to other text that you want to format the same way. The Format Painter is especially useful when you want to copy multiple format settings, but you can also use it to copy individual formats.

QuickTip

Using the Format Painter is not the same as using [F4]. Pressing [F4] repeats only the last action you took. You can use the Format Painter at any time to copy multiple format settings.

7. Select **Events** with the 🖌I pointer, then deselect the text
   Six points of space are added below the Events heading paragraph and the pointer changes back to the I-beam pointer. Compare your document with Figure C-8.

8. Select **Events**, then double-click 🖌
   Double-clicking the Format Painter button allows the Format Painter to remain active until you turn it off. By keeping the Format Painter turned on you can apply formatting to multiple items.

9. Scroll down, select the headings **Classes & Workshops**, **Publications**, and **Surveys** with the 🖌I pointer, then click 🖌 to turn off the Format Painter
   Six points of space are added below each heading paragraph.

10. Press **[Ctrl][Home]**, then click the **Save button** 💾 on the Standard toolbar

FIGURE C-7: Indents and Spacing tab in Paragraph dialog box

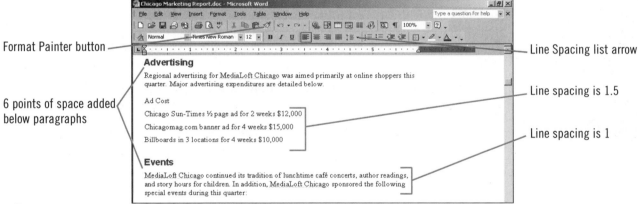

Change the spacing above and below paragraphs

Change the line spacing

Spacing After up arrow

Preview of selected settings

FIGURE C-8: Line and paragraph spacing applied to document

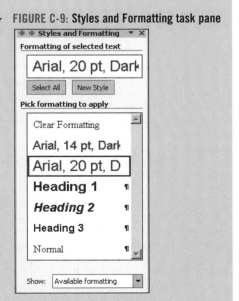

Format Painter button

Line Spacing list arrow

6 points of space added below paragraphs

Line spacing is 1.5

Line spacing is 1

Advertising

Regional advertising for MediaLoft Chicago was aimed primarily at online shoppers this quarter. Major advertising expenditures are detailed below.

Ad Cost

Chicago Sun-Times ½ page ad for 2 weeks $12,000

Chicagomag.com banner ad for 4 weeks $15,000

Billboards in 3 locations for 4 weeks $10,000

Events

MediaLoft Chicago continued its tradition of lunchtime café concerts, author readings, and story hours for children. In addition, MediaLoft Chicago sponsored the following special events during this quarter:

CLUES TO USE

Formatting with styles

You can also apply multiple format settings to text in one step by applying a style. A **style** is a set of formats, such as font, font size, and paragraph alignment, that are named and stored together. To work with styles, click the Styles and Formatting button ⊞ on the Formatting toolbar to open the Styles and Formatting task pane, shown in Figure C-9. The task pane displays the list of available styles and the formats you have created for the current document, if any. To view all the styles available in Word, click the Show list arrow at the bottom of the task pane, then click All Styles.

A **character style**, indicated by a **ₐ** character in the list of styles, includes character format settings, such as font and font size. A **paragraph style**, indicated by a ¶ character in the list, is a combination of character and paragraph formats, such as font, font size, paragraph alignment, and paragraph spacing. To apply a style, select the text or paragraph you want to format, then click the style name in the Pick formatting to apply list box.

FIGURE C-9: Styles and Formatting task pane

Aligning Paragraphs

Changing paragraph alignment is another way to enhance a document's appearance. Paragraphs are aligned relative to the left and right margins in a document. By default, text is **left-aligned**, which means it is flush with the left margin and has a ragged right edge. Using the alignment buttons on the Formatting toolbar, you can **right-align** a paragraph—make it flush with the right margin—or **center** a paragraph so that it is positioned evenly between the left and right margins. You can also **justify** a paragraph so that both the left and right edges of the paragraph are flush with the left and right margins. ✎▬▬ Isaac changes the alignment of several paragraphs at the beginning of the report to make it visually more interesting.

Steps 1 2 3 4

1. Replace **Your Name, Today's Date** with your name, a comma, and the date

2. Select your name and the date, then click the **Align Right button** 🔳 on the Formatting toolbar

    The text is aligned with the right margin. In Normal view, the junction of the white and shaded sections of the horizontal ruler indicates the location of the right margin. The left end of the ruler indicates the left margin.

3. Place the insertion point between your name and the comma, press **[Delete]** to delete the comma, then press **[Enter]**

    The new paragraph containing the date is also right-aligned. Pressing [Enter] in the middle of a paragraph creates a new paragraph with the same text and paragraph formatting as the original paragraph.

4. Select the **report title**, then click the **Center button** 🔳 on the Formatting toolbar

    The two paragraphs that make up the title are centered between the left and right margins.

5. Place the insertion point in the **Advertising** heading, then click 🔳

    The Advertising heading is centered.

6. Place the insertion point in the italicized paragraph under the report title, then click the **Justify button** 🔳

    The paragraph is aligned with both the left and right margins, as shown in Figure C-10. When you justify a paragraph, Word adjusts the spacing between words so that each line in the paragraph is flush with the left and the right margins.

7. Place the insertion point in **MediaLoft** in the report title, click **Format** on the menu bar, then click **Reveal Formatting**

    The Reveal Formatting task pane opens in the Word program window, as shown in Figure C-11. The task pane shows the formatting applied to the text and paragraph where the insertion point is located. You can use the Reveal Formatting task pane to check or change the formatting of any character, word, paragraph, or other aspect of a document.

8. Select **Advertising**, then click the **Alignment** hyperlink in the Reveal Formatting task pane

    The Paragraph dialog box opens with the Indents and Spacing tab displayed. It shows the settings for the selected text.

9. Click the **Alignment list arrow**, click **Left**, click **OK**, then deselect the text

    The Advertising heading is left-aligned.

10. Close the Reveal Formatting task pane, then click the **Save button** 🔳 on the Standard toolbar

FIGURE C-10: Modified paragraph alignment

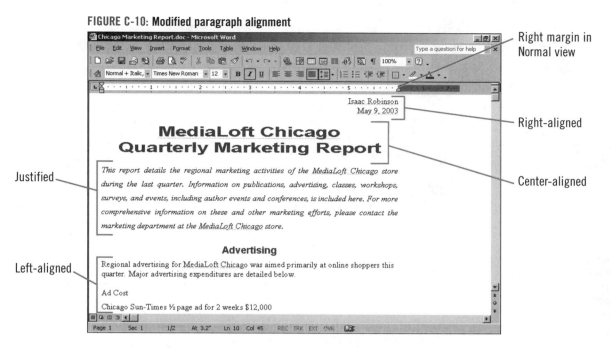

Right margin in Normal view

Right-aligned

Justified

Center-aligned

Left-aligned

FIGURE C-11: Reveal Formatting task pane

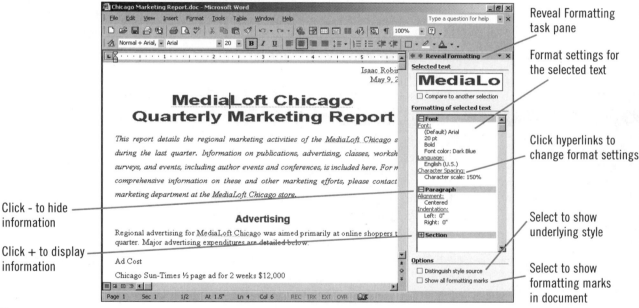

Reveal Formatting task pane

Format settings for the selected text

Click hyperlinks to change format settings

Click - to hide information

Select to show underlying style

Click + to display information

Select to show formatting marks in document

CLUES TO USE

Working with Click and Type

Word's Click and Type feature allows you to automatically apply the paragraph formatting necessary to insert text (or graphics or tables) in a blank area of a document in Print Layout or Web Layout view. As you move the pointer around in a blank area of a document, the pointer changes depending on its location. Double-clicking with a click and type pointer in a blank area of a document automatically applies the appropriate alignment and indentation for that location, so that when you begin typing, the text is already formatted.

The pointer shape indicates which formatting will be applied at each location when you double-click. For example, if you click with the ⥮ pointer, the text you type will be center-aligned. Clicking with ⌶≡ creates a left tab stop at the location of the insertion point so that the text you type is left-aligned at the tab stop. Clicking with ≡⌶ right-aligns the text you type. The ⌶≐ pointer creates left-aligned text with a first line indent. The best way to learn how to use Click and Type is to experiment in a blank document.

Working with Tabs

Tabs allow you to align text vertically at a specific location in a document. A **tab stop** is a point on the horizontal ruler that indicates the location at which to align text. By default, tab stops are located every ½" from the left margin, but you can also set custom tab stops. Using tabs, you can align text to the left, right, or center of a tab stop, or you can align text at a decimal point or bar character. You set tabs using the horizontal ruler or the Tabs command on the Format menu. Isaac uses tabs to format the information on advertising expenditures so it is easy to read.

1. Scroll down until the heading Advertising is at the top of your screen, then select the **four-line list** beginning with Ad Cost
   Before you set tab stops for existing text, you must select the paragraphs for which you want to set tabs.

2. Point to the **tab indicator** ⬜ at the left end of the horizontal ruler
   The icon that appears in the tab indicator indicates the active type of tab; pointing to the tab indicator displays a ScreenTip with the name of the active tab type. By default, left tab is the active tab type. Clicking the tab indicator scrolls through the types of tabs.

3. Click the **tab indicator** to see each of the available tab types, make **left tab** ⬜ the active tab type, then click the **1" mark** on the horizontal ruler
   A left tab stop is inserted at the 1" mark on the horizontal ruler. Clicking the horizontal ruler inserts a tab stop of the active type for the selected paragraph or paragraphs.

4. Click the **tab indicator** twice so the **Right Tab icon** ⬜ is active, then click the **4½" mark** on the horizontal ruler
   A right tab stop is inserted at the 4½" mark on the horizontal ruler, as shown in Figure C-12.

5. Place the insertion point before **Ad** in the first line in the list, press **[Tab]**, place the insertion point before **Cost**, then press **[Tab]**
   Inserting a tab before Ad left-aligns the text at the 1" mark. Inserting a tab before Cost right-aligns Cost at the 4½" mark.

6. Insert a tab at the beginning of each remaining line in the list, then insert a tab before each **$** in the list.
   The paragraphs left-align at the 1" mark. The prices right-align at the 4½" mark.

7. Select the four lines of tabbed text, drag the right tab stop to the **5" mark** on the horizontal ruler, then deselect the text
   Dragging the tab stop moves it to a new location. The prices right-align at the 5" mark.

8. Select the last three lines of tabbed text, click **Format** on the menu bar, then click **Tabs**
   The Tabs dialog box opens, as shown in Figure C-13. You can use the Tabs dialog box to set tab stops, change the position or alignment of existing tab stops, clear tab stops, and apply tab leaders to tabs. **Tab leaders** are lines that appear in front of tabbed text.

9. Click **5"** in the Tab stop position list box, click the **2 option button** in the Leader section, click **OK**, deselect the text, then click the **Save button** ⬜ on the Standard toolbar
   A dotted tab leader is added before each 5" tab stop, as shown in Figure C-14.

FIGURE C-12: Left and right tab stops on the horizontal ruler

Right Tab icon in tab indicator

Left tab stop

Right tab stop

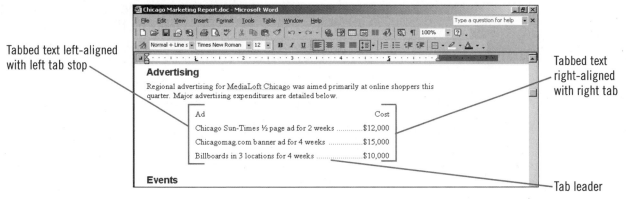

FIGURE C-13: Tabs dialog box

Select the tab stop you want to modify

FIGURE C-14: Tab leaders

Tabbed text left-aligned with left tab stop

Tabbed text right-aligned with right tab

Tab leader

Creating a table

In addition to using tabs to organize text in rows and columns, you can create a table and then enter the text in rows and columns. To create a simple table, place the insertion point where you want to insert the table, click the Insert Table button ⊞ on the Standard toolbar, then, on the grid that appears, drag to select the number of columns and rows you want for the table. When you release the mouse button, an empty table is inserted in the document. To enter or edit text in the table, place the insertion point in a table cell, then type. To move the insertion point from cell to cell, press [Tab] or click in a cell. To format text in a table, select the text, then use the buttons on the Formatting toolbar. The Table menu also includes commands for modifying and formatting tables.

Working with Indents

When you **indent** a paragraph, you move its edge in from the left or right margin. You can indent the entire left or right edge of a paragraph or just the first line. The **indent markers** on the horizontal ruler indicate the indent settings for the paragraph in which the insertion point is located. Dragging the indent markers to a new location on the ruler is one way to change the indentation of a paragraph; using the indent buttons on the Formatting toolbar is another. You can also use the Paragraph command on the Format menu to indent paragraphs. Table C-1 describes different types of indents and the methods for creating each. ✒ Isaac indents several paragraphs in the report.

1. Press **[Ctrl][Home]**, click the **Print Layout View button** 🖹 on the horizontal scroll bar, click the **Zoom list arrow** on the Standard toolbar, then click **Page Width**
   The document is displayed in Print Layout view, making it easier to see the document margins.

QuickTip

Press [Tab] at the beginning of a paragraph to indent the first line ½". You can also set a custom indent using the Indents and Spacing tab in the Paragraph dialog box.

2. Place the insertion point in the italicized paragraph under the title, then click the **Increase Indent button** 📑 on the Formatting toolbar
   The entire paragraph is indented ½" from the left margin, as shown in Figure C-15. The indent marker 🔺 also moves to the ½" mark on the horizontal ruler. Each time you click the Increase Indent button, the left edge of a paragraph moves another ½" to the right.

3. Click the **Decrease Indent button** 📑 on the Formatting toolbar
   The left edge of the paragraph moves ½" to the left, and the indent marker moves back to the left margin.

Trouble?

Take care to drag only the First Line Indent marker. If you make a mistake, click the Undo button 🔙, then try again.

4. Drag the **First Line Indent marker** ▽ to the ¼" mark on the horizontal ruler as shown in Figure C-16
   The first line of the paragraph is indented ¼". Dragging the first line indent marker indents only the first line of a paragraph.

5. Scroll to the bottom of page 1, place the insertion point in the **quote** (the last paragraph), then drag the **Left Indent marker** ▢ to the ½" mark on the horizontal ruler
   When you drag the Left Indent marker, the First Line and Hanging Indent markers move as well. The left edge of the paragraph is indented ½" from the left margin.

6. Drag the **Right Indent marker** △ to the 5½" mark on the horizontal ruler
   The right edge of the paragraph is indented ½" from the right margin, as shown in Figure C-17.

7. Click the **Save button** 🖬 on the Standard toolbar

TABLE C-1: Types of indents

indent type	description	to create
Left indent	The left edge of a paragraph is moved in from the left margin	Drag the Left Indent marker ▢ right to the position where you want the left edge of the paragraph to align, or click the Increase Indent button 📑 to indent the paragraph in ½" increments
Right indent	The right edge of a paragraph is moved in from the right margin	Drag the Right Indent marker △ left to the position where you want the right edge of the paragraph to end
First-line indent	The first line of a paragraph is indented more than the subsequent lines	Drag the First Line Indent marker ▽ right to the position where you want the first line of the paragraph to start
Hanging indent	The subsequent lines of a paragraph are indented more than the first line	Drag the Hanging Indent marker ⬦ right to the position where you want the hanging indent to start
Negative indent (or Outdent)	The left edge of a paragraph is moved to the left of the left margin	Drag the Left Indent marker ▢ left to the position where you want the negative indent to start

FIGURE C-15: Indented paragraph

First Line Indent marker

Hanging Indent marker

Left Indent marker

Indented paragraph

Decrease Indent button

Increase Indent button

Right Indent marker

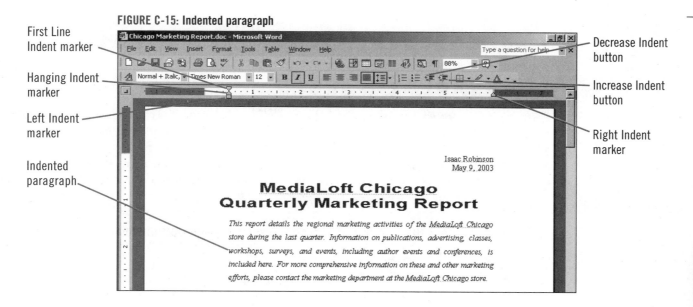

FIGURE C-16: First Line Indent marker being dragged

First Line Indent marker being dragged to the ¼" mark

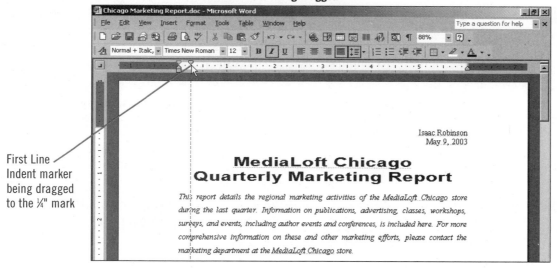

FIGURE C-17: Paragraph indented from the left and right

Paragraph indented ½" from left

Paragraph indented ½" from right

Adding Bullets and Numbering

Formatting a list with bullets or numbering can help to organize the ideas in a document. A **bullet** is a character, often a small circle, that appears before the items in a list to add emphasis. Formatting a list as a numbered list helps illustrate sequences and priorities. You can quickly format a list with bullets or numbering by using the Bullets and Numbering buttons on the Formatting toolbar. You can also use the Bullets and Numbering command on the Format menu to change or customize bullet and numbering styles. ✎ Isaac formats the lists in his report with numbers and bullets.

Steps

1. Scroll down until the first paragraph on the second page (Authors on our…) is at the top of your screen

2. Select the **three-line list of names** under the paragraph, then click the **Numbering button** ▤ on the Formatting toolbar
   The paragraphs are formatted as a numbered list.

3. Place the insertion point after **Jack Seneschal**, press **[Enter]**, then type **Polly Flanagan**
   Pressing [Enter] in the middle of the numbered list creates a new numbered paragraph and automatically renumbers the remainder of the list. Similarly, if you delete a paragraph from a numbered list, Word automatically renumbers the remaining paragraphs.

4. Click **1** in the list
   Clicking a number in a list selects all the numbers, as shown in Figure C-18.

5. Click the **Bold button** ▣ on the Formatting toolbar
   The numbers are all formatted in bold. Notice that the formatting of the items in the list does not change when you change the formatting of the numbers. You can also use this technique to change the formatting of bullets in a bulleted list.

6. Select the **list of classes and workshops** under the Classes & Workshops heading, scrolling down if necessary, then click the **Bullets button** ▤ on the Formatting toolbar
   The five paragraphs are formatted as a bulleted list.

7. With the list still selected, click **Format** on the menu bar, then click **Bullets and Numbering**
   The Bullets and Numbering dialog box opens with the Bulleted tab displayed, as shown in Figure C-19. You use this dialog box to apply bullets and numbering to paragraphs, or to change the style of bullets or numbers.

8. Click the **Square bullets box** or select another style if square bullets are not available to you, click **OK**, then deselect the text
   The bullet character changes to a small square, as shown in Figure C-20.

9. Click the **Save button** ▣ on the Standard toolbar

> **QuickTip**
> To change the numbers to letters, Roman numerals, or another numbering style, right-click the list, click Bullets and Numbering, then select a new numbering style on the Numbered tab.

> **QuickTip**
> To remove a bullet or number, select the paragraph(s), then click ▤ or ▤.

FIGURE C-18: Numbered list

Numbers selected in numbered list

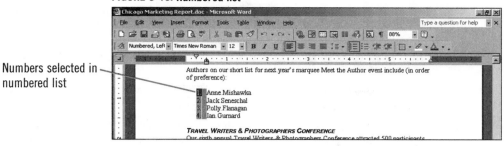

FIGURE C-19: Bulleted tab in the Bullets and Numbering dialog box

Numbered tab contains options for numbered lists

Outline Numbered tab contains options for outlines

Square bullets (your bullet styles might differ)

Click to select different characters and pictures to use as bullets

FIGURE C-20: Square bullets applied to list

Numbers are bold

Square bullets applied to list

Creating outlines

You can create lists with hierarchical structures by applying an outline numbering style to a list. To create an outline, begin by applying an outline numbering style from the Outline Numbered tab in the Bullets and Numbering dialog box, then type your outline, pressing [Enter] after each item. To demote items to a lower level of importance in the outline, place the insertion point in the item, then click the Increase Indent button ▣ on the Formatting toolbar. Each time you indent a paragraph, the item is demoted to a lower lever in the outline. Similarly, you can use the Decrease Indent button ▣ to promote an item to a higher level in the outline. You can also create a hierarchical structure in any bulleted or numbered list by using ▣ and ▣ to demote and promote items in the list. To change the outline numbering style applied to a list, select a new style from the Outline Numbered tab in the Bullets and Numbering dialog box.

Adding Borders and Shading

Borders and shading can add color and splash to a document. **Borders** are lines you add above, below, to the side, or around words or a paragraph. You can format borders using different line styles, colors, and widths. **Shading** is a color or pattern you apply behind words or paragraphs to make them stand out on a page. You apply borders and shading using the Borders and Shading command on the Format menu. ✒ Isaac enhances the advertising expenses table by adding shading to it. He also applies a border under every heading to visually punctuate the sections of the report.

Steps 1234

1. Scroll up until the heading Advertising is at the top of your screen

2. Select the **four paragraphs** of tabbed text under the Advertising heading, click **Format** on the menu bar, click **Borders and Shading**, then click the **Shading tab**
   The Shading tab in the Borders and Shading dialog box is shown in Figure C-21. You use this tab to apply shading to words and paragraphs.

3. Click the **Pale Blue box** in the bottom row of the Fill section, click **OK**, then deselect the text
   Pale blue shading is applied to the four paragraphs. Notice that the shading is applied to the entire width of the paragraphs, despite the tab settings.

4. Select the **four paragraphs**, drag the **Left Indent marker** ⬜ to the ¾" mark on the horizontal ruler, drag the **Right Indent marker** △ to the 5¼" mark, then deselect the text
   The paragraphs are indented from the left and right, making the shading look more attractive.

5. Select **Advertising**, click **Format** on the menu bar, click **Borders and Shading**, then click the **Borders tab**
   The Borders tab is shown in Figure C-22. You use this tab to add boxes and lines to words or paragraphs.

QuickTip

When creating custom borders, it's important to select the style, color, and width settings before applying the borders in the Preview section.

6. Click the **Custom box** in the Setting section, click the **Width list arrow**, click ¾ pt, click the **Bottom Border button** ▦ in the Preview section, click **OK**, then deselect the text
   A ¾-point black border is added below the Advertising paragraph.

7. Click **Events**, press **[F4]**, then scroll down and use **[F4]** to add a border under each blue heading
   The completed document is shown in Figure C-23.

Trouble?

Adjust the colors in the document if necessary.

8. Click the **Save button** 🖫 on the Standard toolbar, click the **Print button** 🖨, close the document, then exit Word
   A copy of the report prints. Depending on your printer, colors might appear differently when you print. If you are using a black and white printer, colors will print in shades of gray.

CLUES TO USE

Highlighting text in a document

You can mark important text in a document with highlighting. **Highlighting** is transparent color that is applied to text using the Highlight pointer ✐. To highlight text, click the Highlight list arrow ✐▾ on the Formatting toolbar, select a color, then use the I-beam part of the ✐ pointer to select the text. Click ✐ to turn off the Highlight pointer. To remove highlighting, select the highlighted text, click ✐▾, then click None. Highlighting prints, but it is used most effectively when a document is viewed online.

FIGURE C-21: Shading tab in Borders and Shading dialog box

Name of active color appears here

Pale Blue

Click to select a shading pattern

Preview of shading settings

Click to choose to apply the settings to the paragraph or to the selected text

FIGURE C-22: Borders tab in Borders and Shading dialog box

Select border formats before applying them in the Preview section

Select Custom to add a single border

Preview of border settings

Bottom border button

Click buttons or edges of preview to apply individual borders

FIGURE C-23: Borders and shading applied to the document

Border under headings

Shading applied to paragraphs

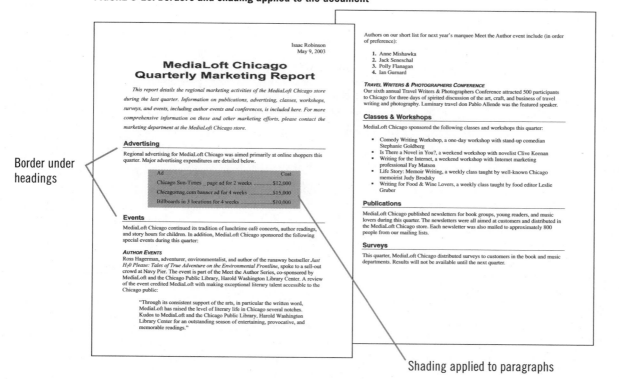

Practice

► Concepts Review

Label each element of the Word program window shown in Figure C-24.

FIGURE C-24

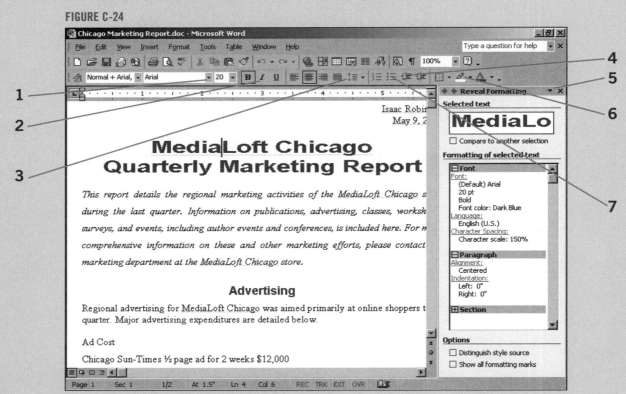

Match each term with the statement that best describes it.

- 8. **Italic**
- 9. **Bullet**
- 10. **Style**
- 11. **Bold**
- 12. **Point**
- 13. **Highlight**
- 14. **Shading**
- 15. **Border**

- a. A character that appears at the beginning of a paragraph to add emphasis
- b. Transparent color that is applied to text to mark it in a document
- c. A text style in which characters are slanted
- d. Color or a pattern that is applied behind text to make it look attractive
- e. A set of format settings
- f. A unit of measurement equal to ½ of an inch
- g. A line that can be applied above, below, or to the sides of a paragraph
- h. A text style in which characters are darker and thicker

Select the best answer from the list of choices.

16. Which button is used to align a paragraph with both the left and right margins?

a. ▦
b. ▦
c. ▦
d. ▦

17. What is Times New Roman?
   a. A character format
   b. A font
   c. A style
   d. A text effect

18. What is the most precise way to increase the amount of white space between two paragraphs?
   a. Indent the paragraphs.
   b. Insert an extra blank line between the paragraphs.
   c. Use the Paragraph command to change the spacing below the first paragraph.
   d. Change the line spacing of the paragraphs.

19. What element of the Word program window can be used to check the font effects applied to text?
   a. Standard toolbar
   b. Formatting toolbar
   c. Styles and Formatting task pane
   d. Reveal Formatting task pane

20. Which command would you use to apply color behind a paragraph?
   a. Borders and Shading
   b. Background
   c. Paragraph
   d. Styles and Formatting

▶ Skills Review

1. Format with fonts.
   a. Start Word, open the file WD C-2 from the drive and folder where your Project Files are located, save it as **EDA Report**, then scroll through the document to get a feel for its contents.
   b. Press [Ctrl][Home], format the report title **Concord Springs Economic Development Report Executive Summary** in 22-point Tahoma. Choose a different font if Tahoma is not available to you.
   c. Change the font color of the report title to Blue-Gray.
   d. Format each of the following headings in 14-point Tahoma with the Blue-Gray font color: **Mission Statement**, **Guiding Principles**, **Issues**, **Proposed Actions**.
   e. Press [Ctrl][Home], then save your changes to the report.

2. Change font styles and effects.
   a. Apply bold to the report title and to each heading in the report.
   b. Format the paragraph under the Mission Statement heading in italic.
   c. Format the third paragraph under the Issues heading, **Years Population Growth**, in bold small caps, with a Blue-Gray font color.
   d. Change the font color of the two paragraphs under Years Population Growth to Blue-Gray.
   e. Format the paragraph **Source: Office of State Planning** in italic.
   f. Scroll to the top of the report, change the character scale of **Concord Springs Economic Development Report** to 80%, then save your changes.

3. Change line and paragraph spacing.
   a. Change the line spacing of the three-line list under the first body paragraph to 1.5 lines.
   b. Add 12 points of space before the Executive Summary paragraph.
   c. Add 12 points of space after each heading in the report.
   d. Add 6 points of space after each paragraph in the list under the Guiding Principles heading.
   e. Add 6 points of space after each paragraph under the Proposed Actions heading.
   f. Press [Ctrl][Home], then save your changes to the report.

4. Align paragraphs.

a. Press [Ctrl][A] to select the entire document, then justify all the paragraphs.

b. Center the two-paragraph report title.

c. Press [Ctrl][End], type your name, press [Enter], type the current date, then right-align your name and the date.

d. Save your changes to the report.

5. Work with tabs.

a. Scroll up and select the four-line list of blue-gray population information.

b. Set left tab stops at the 1¾"-mark and the 3" mark.

c. Insert a tab at the beginning of each paragraph in the list.

d. In the first paragraph, insert a tab before Population. In the second paragraph, insert a tab before 4.5%. In the third paragraph, insert a tab before 53%.

e. Select the first three paragraphs, then drag the second tab stop to the 2¾" mark on the horizontal ruler.

f. Press [Ctrl][Home], then save your changes to the report.

6. Work with indents.

a. Indent the first line of the first body paragraph ½".

b. Indent the paragraph under the Mission Statement heading ½" from the left and ½" from the right.

c. Indent the first line of the paragraph under the Guiding Principles heading ½".

d. Indent the first line of the three body paragraphs under the Issues heading ½".

e. Press [Ctrl][Home], then save your changes to the report.

7. Add bullets and numbering.

a. Apply bullets to the three-line list under the first body paragraph.

b. Change the bullet style to small circles (or choose another bullet style if small circles are not available to you).

c. Change the font color of the bullets to Blue-Gray.

d. Scroll down until the Guiding Principles heading is at the top of your screen.

e. Format the five-paragraph list under Guiding Principles as a numbered list.

f. Format the numbers in 12-point Tahoma bold, then change the font color to Blue-Gray.

g. Scroll down until the Proposed Actions heading is at the top of your screen, then format the paragraphs under the heading as a bulleted list using checkmarks as the bullet style (or choose another bullet style).

h. Change the font color of the bullets to Blue-Gray, press [Ctrl][Home], then save your changes to the report.

8. Add borders and shading.

a. Change the font color of the report title to Light Yellow, then apply Blue-Gray shading.

b. Apply Light Yellow shading to the Mission Statement heading, then add a 1-point Blue-Gray border below the Mission Statement heading.

c. Use the Format Painter to copy the formatting of the Mission Statement heading to the other headings in the report.

d. Under the Issues heading, select the first three lines of tabbed text, which are formatted in Blue-Gray.

e. Apply Light Yellow shading to the paragraphs, then add a 1-point Blue-Gray box border around the paragraphs.

f. Indent the paragraphs 1½" from the left and 1½" from the right.

g. Press [Ctrl][Home], save your changes to the report, view the report in Print Preview, then print a copy. The formatted report is shown in Figure C-25.

h. Close the file and exit Word.

FIGURE C-25

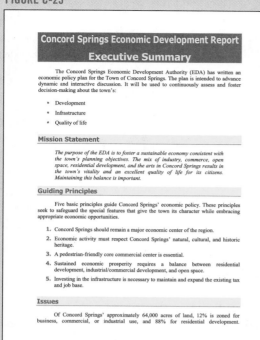

► Independent Challenge 1

You are an estimator for Zakia Construction in the Australian city of Wollongong. You have drafted an estimate for a home renovation job, and need to format it. It's important that your estimate have a clean, striking design, and reflect your company's professionalism.

FIGURE C-26

ZAKIAConstruction

73 Corrimal Street
Wollongong, NSW 2500
Tel: 02-4225-3202
www.zabel.com.au

a. Start Word, open the file WD C-3 from the drive and folder where your Project Files are located, save it as **Zakia Construction**, then read the document to get a feel for its contents. Figure C-26 shows how you will format the letterhead.

b. In the first paragraph, format **ZAKIA** in 24-point Arial Black. (*Hint*: Select a similar font if Arial Black is not available to you.)

c. Format **Construction** in 24-point Arial, then change the character scale to 90%.

d. Format the next four lines in 9-point Arial, right-align them, then add a 1-point border below the last line.

e. In the body of the document, format the title **Proposal of Renovation** in 16-point Arial Black, then center the title.

f. Format the following headings (including the colons) in 12-point Arial Black: **Date**, **Work to be performed for and at**, **Scope of work**, **Payment schedule** and **Agreement**.

g. Format the 14-paragraph list under Scope of work as a numbered list, then apply bold to the numbers.

h. Change the paragraph spacing to add 4 points of space after each paragraph in the list.

i. With the list selected, set a right tab stop at the 5¾" mark, then insert tabs before every price in the list.

j. Apply bold to the two paragraphs—**Total estimated job cost** and **Approximate job time**—below the list.

k. Replace Your Name with your name in the signature block, select the signature block, set a left tab stop at the 3½" mark, then indent the signature block.

l. Examine the document carefully for formatting errors and make any necessary adjustments.

m. Save and print the document, then close the file and exit Word.

Independent Challenge 2

Your employer, The Lange Center for Contemporary Arts in Halifax, Nova Scotia, is launching a membership drive. Your boss has written the text for a flyer advertising Lange membership, and asks you to format it so that it is eye-catching and attractive.

a. Open the file WD C-4 from the drive and folder where your Project Files are located, save it as **Membership Flyer**, then read the document. Figure C-27 shows how you will format the first several paragraphs of the flyer.

FIGURE C-27

MEMBERSHIP DRIVE
2003

What we do for ARTISTS
Since 1982, the artist residency program at the Lange Center for Contemporary Arts has supported the work of more than 1500 artists from all over Canada and from 40 other nations. The residency awards include studio and living space, a monthly stipend to help artists with their expenses, and use of specialized equipment for all types of visual and performance art. Each artist gives a public lecture or performance at the Lange.

b. Select the entire document and format it in 10-point Arial Narrow.

c. Format the first paragraph, **Membership Drive**, in 26-point Arial Narrow, bold, with a white font color. Expand the character spacing by 7 points. Center the paragraph and apply plum shading to the paragraph.

d. Format the second paragraph, **2003**, in 36-point Arial Black, 80% gray font color, with a shadow effect. Expand the character spacing by 25 points and change the character scale to 200%. Center the paragraph.

e. Format each **What we do for…** heading in 12-point Arial, bold, with a plum font color. Add a single line ½-point border under each heading.

f. Format each subheading (**Gallery, Lectures, Library, All members…**, and **Membership Levels**) in 10-point Arial, bold. Add 3 points of spacing before each paragraph.

g. Indent each body paragraph ¼", except for the paragraphs under the What we do for YOU heading.

h. Format the four paragraphs under the All members… subheading as a bulleted list. Use a bullet symbol of your choice and format the bullets in the plum color.

i. Indent the five paragraphs under the Membership Levels heading ¼". For these five paragraphs, set left tab stops at the 1¼" mark and the 2" mark on the horizontal ruler. Insert tabs before the price and before the word **All** in each of the five paragraphs.

j. Format the name of each membership level (**Artistic, Conceptual**, etc.) in 10-point Arial, bold, italic, with a plum font color.

k. Format the **For more information** paragraph in 14-point Arial, bold, with a plum font color. Center the paragraph and add a 6-point dotted black border above the paragraph.

l. Format the last two paragraphs in 11-point Arial Narrow, and center the paragraphs. In the contact information, replace **Your Name** with your name, then apply bold to your name.

m. Examine the document carefully for formatting errors and make any necessary adjustments.

n. Save and print the flyer, then close the file and exit Word.

► Independent Challenge 3

One of your responsibilities as program coordinator at Solstice Mountain Sports is to develop a program of winter outdoor learning and adventure workshops. You have written a memo to your boss to update her on your progress. You need to format the memo so it is professional-looking and easy to read.

a. Start Word, open the file WD C-5 from the drive and folder where your Project Files are located, then save it as **Solstice Memo**.

b. Format the heading **Solstice Mountain Sports Memorandum** in 26-point Impact, then center it.

c. In the memo header, replace Today's Date and Your Name with the current date and your name.

d. Select the four-line memo header, set a left tab stop at the ¾" mark, then insert tabs before the date, the recipient's name, your name, and the subject of the memo.

e. Select **Date:**, then apply the character style Strong to it. FIGURE C-28
(*Hint:* Open the Styles and Formatting task pane, click the Show list arrow, click All Styles if necessary, scroll through the alphabetical list of styles to locate the style Strong, then click Strong.)

f. Apply the Strong style to **To:**, **From:**, and **Re:**, then double-space the four lines in the memo header.

g. Apply a 3-point dotted border below the blank line under the memo header. (*Hint:* Turn on formatting marks, select the paragraph symbol below the memo header, then apply a border below it.)

h. Apply the paragraph style Heading 3 to the headings **Overview**, **Workshops**, **Accommodation**, **Fees**, and **Proposed winter programming**.

i. Under the Fees heading, format the words **Workshop fees** and **Accommodation fees** using the Strong style.

j. Add 6 points of space after the Workshop fees paragraph.

k. In the Fees section, apply green highlighting to these sentences: **Workshop fees include materials and equipment.** and **This is a discounted rate.**

l. On the second page of the document, format the list under the Proposed winter programming heading as an outline. Figure C-28 shows the hierarchical structure of the outline. (*Hint:* Format the list as an outline numbered list, then use the Increase Indent and Decrease Indent buttons to change the level of importance of each item.)

m. Change the outline numbering style to the bullet numbering style shown in Figure C-28, if necessary.

n. Save and print the document, then close the file and exit Word.

Proposed winter programming
- ❖ Skiing, Snowboarding, and Snowshoeing
  - ➢ Skiing and Snowboarding
    - ▪ Cross-country skiing
      - • Cross-country skiing for beginners
      - • Intermediate cross-country skiing
      - • Inn-to-inn ski touring
      - • Moonlight cross-country skiing
    - ▪ Telemarking
      - • Basic telemark skiing
      - • Introduction to backcountry skiing
      - • Exploring on skis
    - ▪ Snowboarding
      - • Backcountry snowboarding
  - ➢ Snowshoeing
    - ▪ Beginner
      - • Snowshoeing for beginners
      - • Snowshoeing and winter ecology
    - ▪ Intermediate and Advanced
      - • Intermediate snowshoeing
      - • Guided snowshoe trek
      - • Above tree line snowshoeing
- ❖ Winter Hiking, Camping, and Survival
  - ➢ Hiking
    - ▪ Beginner
      - • Long-distance hiking
      - • Winter summits
      - • Hiking for women
  - ➢ Winter camping and survival
    - ▪ Beginner
      - • Introduction to winter camping
      - • Basic winter mountain skills
      - • Building snow shelters
    - ▪ Intermediate
      - • Basic winter mountain skills II
      - • Ice climbing
      - • Avalanche awareness and rescue

Independent Challenge 4

The fonts you choose for a document can have a major effect on the document's tone. Not all fonts are appropriate for use in a business document, and some fonts, especially those with a definite theme, are appropriate only for specific purposes. The World Wide Web includes hundreds of Web sites devoted to fonts and text design. Some Web sites sell fonts, others allow you to download fonts for free and install them on your computer. In this independent challenge, you will research Web sites related to fonts and find examples of fonts you could use in your work.

a. Start Word, open the file WD C-6 from the drive and folder where your Project Files are located, and save it as **Fonts**. This document contains the questions you will answer about the fonts you find.

b. Use your favorite search engine to search the Web for Web sites related to fonts. Use the keyword **font** to conduct your search. If your search does not result in appropriate links, try looking at the following Web sites: www.1001freefonts.com, www.fontsnthings.com, and www.fontfreak.com.

c. Explore the fonts available for downloading. As you examine the fonts, notice that fonts fall into two general categories: serif fonts, which have a small stroke, called a serif, at the ends of characters, and sans serif fonts, which do not have a serif. Times New Roman is an example of a serif font and Arial is an example of a sans serif font.

d. Type your answers in the Fonts document, save it, print a copy, then close the file and exit Word.

Word 2002

► Visual Workshop

Using the file WD C-7 found in the drive and folder where your Project Files are located, create the menu shown in Figure C-29. (*Hints*: Use Georgia for the font. Change the font size of the heading to 72 points, scale the font to 66%, and expand the spacing by 2 points. For the rest of the text, change the font size to 11 points. Indent all the text ½" from the left and the right. Use paragraph spacing to adjust the spacing between paragraphs so that all the text fits on one page. If the Georgia font is not available to you, choose a different font.) Save the menu as **Rosebud Specials**, then print a copy.

FIGURE C-29

Rosebud Café

. . . . .

DAILY SPECIALS

MONDAY
Veggie Chili
Hearty veggie chili with melted cheddar in our peasant French bread bowl. Topped with sour cream & scallions.
$5.95

TUESDAY
Greek Salad
Our large garden salad with kalamata olives, feta cheese, and garlic vinaigrette. Served with an assortment of rolls.
$5.95

WEDNESDAY
French Dip
Lean roast beef topped with melted cheddar on our roasted garlic roll. Served with a side of au jus and red bliss mashed potatoes.
$6.95

THURSDAY
Chicken Cajun Bleu
Cajun chicken, chunky blue cheese, cucumbers, leaf lettuce, and tomato on our roasted garlic roll.
$6.50

FRIDAY
Clam Chowder
Classic New England thick, rich, clam chowder in our peasant French bread bowl. Served with a garden salad.
$5.95

SATURDAY
Hot Chicken and Gravy
Delicious chicken and savory gravy served on a thick slice of toasted honest white. Served with red bliss mashed potatoes.
$6.95

SUNDAY
Turkey-Bacon Club
Double-decker roasted turkey, crisp bacon, leaf lettuce, tomato, and sun-dried tomato mayo on toasted triple seed.
$6.50

Your Name
. . . . .

Unit
D

Formatting
Documents

- ⌐MOUS⌐ ► **Set document margins**
- ⌐MOUS⌐ ► **Divide a document into sections**
- ⌐MOUS⌐ ► **Add page breaks**
- ⌐MOUS⌐ ► **Add page numbers**
- ⌐MOUS⌐ ► **Insert headers and footers**
- ⌐MOUS⌐ ► **Edit headers and footers**
- ⌐MOUS⌐ ► **Format columns**
- ⌐MOUS⌐ ► **Insert clip art**

Word's page formatting features allow you to creatively lay out and design the pages of your documents. In this unit, you learn how to change the document margins, determine the page orientation of a document, add page numbers, and insert headers and footers. You also learn how to format text in columns and how to illustrate your documents with clip art. ✐ Alice Wegman has written and formatted the text for a quarterly newsletter for the MediaLoft marketing staff. She is now ready to lay out and design the pages of the newsletter. She plans to organize the articles in columns and to illustrate the newsletter with clip art. You will work with Alice as she formats the newsletter.

Setting Document Margins

Changing a document's margins is one way to change the appearance of a document and control the amount of text that fits on a page. The **margins** of a document are the blank areas between the edge of the text and the edge of the page. When you create a document in Word, the default margins are 1" at the top and bottom of the page, and 1.25" on the left and right sides of the page. You can adjust the size of a document's margins using the Page Setup command on the File menu, or using the rulers. Alice plans the newsletter to be a four-page document when finished. She reduces the size of the document margins so that more text fits on each page.

Steps 1 2 3 4

1. Start **Word**, open the file **WD D-1** from the drive and folder where your Project Files are located, then save it as **MediaLoft Buzz**
   The newsletter opens in Print Layout view.

2. Scroll through the newsletter to get a feel for its contents, then press **[Ctrl][Home]**
   The newsletter is currently six pages long. Notice the status bar indicates the page where the insertion point is located and the total number of pages in the document.

3. Click **File** on the menu bar, click **Page Setup**, then click the **Margins tab** in the Page Setup dialog box if necessary
   The Margins tab in the Page Setup dialog box is shown in Figure D-1. You can use the Margins tab to change the width of the top, bottom, left, or right document margins, to change the orientation of the pages from portrait to landscape, and to alter other page layout settings. **Portrait orientation** means a page is taller than it is wide; **landscape orientation** means a page is wider than it is tall. This newsletter uses portrait orientation.

4. Click the **Top down arrow** three times until 0.7" appears, then click the **Bottom down arrow** until 0.7" appears
   The top and bottom margins of the newsletter will be .7". Notice that the margins in the Preview section of the dialog box change as you adjust the margin settings.

5. Press **[Tab]**, type **.7** in the Left text box, press **[Tab]**, then type **.7** in the Right text box
   The left and right margins of the newsletter will also be .7". You can change the margin settings by using the arrows or by typing a value in the appropriate text box.

6. Click **OK**
   The document margins change to .7", as shown in Figure D-2. The bar at the intersection of the white and gray areas on the horizontal and vertical rulers indicates the location of the margin. You can also change a document's margins by dragging the bar to a new location. Notice that the status bar indicates the total number of pages in the document is now five.

7. Click the **Zoom list arrow** on the Standard toolbar, then click **Two Pages**
   The first two pages of the document appear in the document window.

8. Scroll down to view all five pages of the newsletter, press **[Ctrl][Home]**, click the **Zoom list arrow**, click **Page Width**, then click the **Save button** on the Standard toolbar to save the document

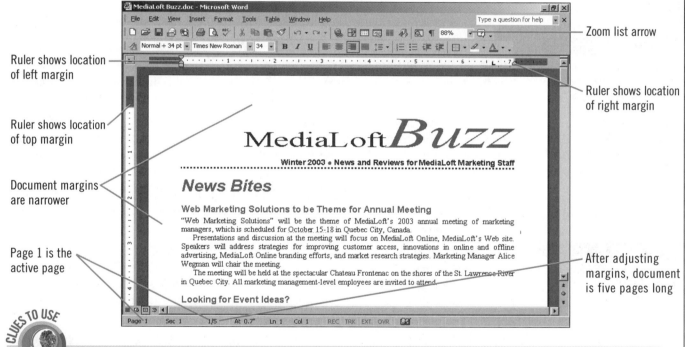

FIGURE D-1: Margins tab in Page Setup dialog box

Default margin settings

Set gutter margin

Select page orientation

Select part of document to apply settings to

Select gutter position

Set mirror margins and other page layout options

Preview of margin settings

FIGURE D-2: Newsletter with smaller margins

Ruler shows location of left margin

Ruler shows location of top margin

Document margins are narrower

Page 1 is the active page

Zoom list arrow

Ruler shows location of right margin

After adjusting margins, document is five pages long

MediaLoft *Buzz*

Winter 2003 ● News and Reviews for MediaLoft Marketing Staff

News Bites

Web Marketing Solutions to be Theme for Annual Meeting

"Web Marketing Solutions" will be the theme of MediaLoft's 2003 annual meeting of marketing managers, which is scheduled for October 15-18 in Quebec City, Canada.

Presentations and discussion at the meeting will focus on MediaLoft Online, MediaLoft's Web site. Speakers will address strategies for improving customer access, innovations in online and offline advertising, MediaLoft Online branding efforts, and market research strategies. Marketing Manager Alice Wegman will chair the meeting.

The meeting will be held at the spectacular Chateau Frontenac on the shores of the St. Lawrence River in Quebec City. All marketing management-level employees are invited to attend.

Looking for Event Ideas?

CLUES TO USE

Changing paper size, orientation, and margin settings

By default, the documents you create in Word use an 8½" x 11" paper size in portrait orientation with the default margin settings, but you can adjust these settings in the Page Setup dialog box to create documents of any size, shape, and layout. On the Margins tab, change the orientation of the pages by selecting Portrait or Landscape. To change the layout of multiple pages, use the Multiple pages list arrow to create pages that use mirror margins, include two pages per sheet of paper, or are formatted like a folded booklet. **Mirror margins** are used in documents with facing pages, such as a magazine, where the margins on the left page of the document are a mirror image of the margins on

the right. Documents with mirror margins have inside and outside margins, rather than right and left margins. Another type of margin is a gutter margin, which is used in documents that are bound, such as books. A **gutter** adds extra space to the left or top margin so that the binding does not obscure text. Add a gutter to a document by adjusting the setting in the Gutter text box on the Margins tab. If you want to change the size of the paper used in a document, use the Paper tab in the Page Setup dialog box. Use the Paper size list arrow to select a standard paper size, or enter custom measurements in the Width and Height text boxes.

Word 2002

Dividing a Document into Sections

Dividing a document into sections allows you to format each section of the document with different page layout settings. A **section** is a portion of a document that is separated from the rest of the document by section breaks. **Section breaks** are formatting marks that you insert in a document to show the end of a section. Once you have divided a document into sections, you can format each section with different column, margin, page orientation, header and footer, and other page layout settings. By default, a document is formatted as a single section, but you can divide a document into as many sections as you like. Alice wants to format the body of the newsletter in two columns, but leave the masthead and the headline "News Bites" as a single column. She inserts a section break before the body of the newsletter to divide the document into two sections, then she changes the number of columns in the second section to two.

1. **Click the Show/Hide ¶ button ¶ on the Standard toolbar to display formatting marks if they are not visible**
   Turning on formatting marks allows you to see the section breaks you insert in a document.

2. **Place the insertion point before the headline Web Marketing Solutions to be..., click Insert on the menu bar, then click Break**
   The Break dialog box opens, as shown in Figure D-3. You use this dialog box to insert different types of section breaks. Table D-1 describes the different types of section breaks.

QuickTip

When you insert a section break at the beginning of a paragraph, Word inserts the break at the end of the previous paragraph. A section break stores the formatting information for the preceding section.

3. **Click the Continuous option button, then click OK**
   Word inserts a continuous section break, shown as a dotted double line, above the headline. A continuous section break begins a new section of the document on the same page. The document now has two sections. Notice that the status bar indicates that the insertion point is in section 2.

4. **With the insertion point in section 2, click the Columns button ▦ on the Standard toolbar**
   A grid showing four columns opens below the button. You use the grid to select the number of columns you want to create.

QuickTip

To change the margins or page orientation of a section, place the insertion point in the section, change the margin or page orientation settings on the Margins tab in the Page Setup dialog box, click the Apply to list arrow on the Margins tab, click This section, then click OK.

5. **Point to the second column on the grid, then click**
   Section 2 is formatted in two columns, as shown in Figure D-4. The text in section 1 remains formatted in a single column. Notice the status bar now indicates the document is four pages long. Formatting text in columns is another way to increase the amount of text that fits on a page. You'll learn more about columns in a later lesson.

6. **Click the Zoom list arrow on the Standard toolbar, click Two Pages, then scroll down to examine all four pages of the document**
   The text in section 2—all the text below the continuous section break—is formatted in two columns. Text in columns flows automatically from the bottom of one column to the top of the next.

7. **Press [Ctrl][Home], click the Zoom list arrow, click Page Width, then save the document**

TABLE D-1: Types of section breaks

section break	function
Next page	Begins a new a section and moves the text following the break to the top of the next page
Continuous	Begins a new section on the same page
Even page	Begins a new section and moves the text following the break to the top of the next even-numbered page
Odd page	Begins a new section and moves the text following the break to the top of the next odd-numbered page

FIGURE D-3: Break dialog box

FIGURE D-4: Continuous section break and columns

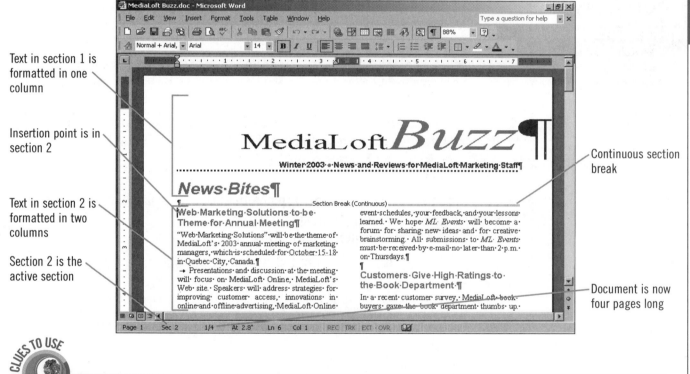

Text in section 1 is formatted in one column

Insertion point is in section 2

Text in section 2 is formatted in two columns

Section 2 is the active section

Continuous section break

Document is now four pages long

CLUES TO USE

Changing page layout settings for a section

Dividing a document into sections allows you to vary the layout of a document. In addition to applying different column settings to sections, you can apply different margins, page orientation, paper size, vertical alignment, header and footer, page numbering, and other page layout settings. For example, if you are formatting a report that includes a table with many columns, you might want to change the table's page orientation to landscape so that it is easier to read. To do this, you would insert a section break before and after the table to create a section that contains only the table. Then you would use the Margins tab in the Page Setup dialog box to change the page orientation of the table section to landscape.

To change the page layout settings for an individual section, place the insertion point in the section, open the Page Setup (or Columns) dialog box, select the options you want to change, click the Apply to list arrow, click This section, then click OK. When you select This section in the Apply to list box, the settings are applied to the current section only. If you select Whole document in the Apply to list box, the settings are applied to all the sections in the document.

Adding Page Breaks

As you type text in a document, Word automatically inserts a **soft page break** when you reach the bottom of a page, allowing you to continue typing on the next page. You can also force text onto the next page of a document by using the Break command to insert a **hard page break**. Alice inserts hard page breaks where she knows she wants to begin each new page of the newsletter.

Steps

1. Scroll down to the bottom of page 1, place the insertion point before the headline **Career Corner**, click **Insert** on the menu bar, then click **Break**

   The Break dialog box opens. You also use this dialog box to insert page, column, and text-wrapping breaks. Table D-2 describes these types of breaks.

2. Make sure the **Page break option button** is selected, then click **OK**

   Word inserts a hard page break before "Career Corner" and moves all the text following the page break to the beginning of the next page, as shown in Figure D-5. The page break appears as a dotted line in Print Layout view. Page break marks are visible on the screen but do not print.

3. Scroll down to the bottom of page 2, place the insertion point before the headline **Webcasts Slated for May**, press and hold **[Ctrl]**, then press **[Enter]**

   Pressing [Ctrl][Enter] is a fast way to insert a hard page break. The headline is forced to the top of the third page.

4. Scroll down to the bottom of page 3, place the insertion point before the headline **Staff News**, then press **[Ctrl][Enter]**

   The headline is forced to the top of the fourth page.

5. Press **[Ctrl][Home]**, click the **Zoom list arrow** on the Standard toolbar, then click **Two Pages**

   The first two pages of the document are displayed, as shown in Figure D-6.

6. Scroll down to view pages 3 and 4, click the **Zoom list arrow**, click **Page Width**, then save the document

Vertically aligning text on a page

By default, text is vertically aligned with the top margin of a page, but you can change the vertical alignment of text so that it is centered between the top and bottom margins, justified between the top and bottom margins, or aligned with the bottom margin of the page. You would vertically align text on a page only when the text does not fill the page; for example, if you are creating a flyer or a title page for a report. To change the vertical alignment of text in a section (or a document), place the insertion point in the section you want to align, open the Page Setup dialog box, use the Vertical alignment list arrow on the Layout tab to select the alignment you want—top, center, justified, or bottom—use the Apply to list arrow to select the part of the document you want to align, then click OK.

FIGURE D-5: Hard page break in document

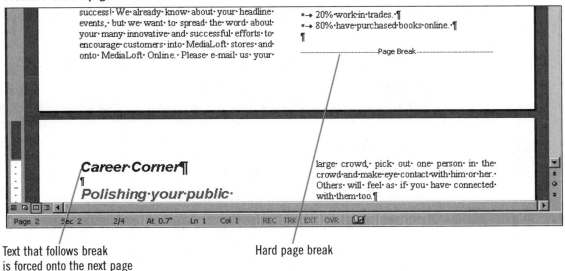

Text that follows break
is forced onto the next page

Hard page break

FIGURE D-6: Pages 1 and 2

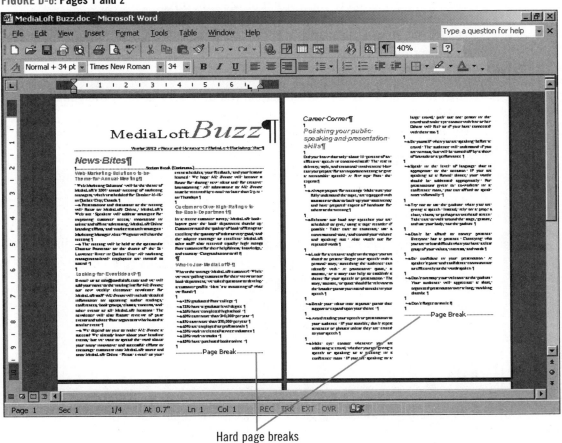

Hard page breaks

TABLE D-2: Types of breaks

break	function
Page break	Forces the text following the break to begin at the top of the next page
Column break	Forces the text following the break to begin at the top of the next column
Text wrapping break	Forces the text following the break to begin at the beginning of the next line

Adding Page Numbers

If you want to number the pages of a multi-page document, you can insert a page number field at the top or bottom of each page. A **field** is a code that serves as a placeholder for data that changes in a document, such as a page number or the current date. When you use the Page Numbers command on the Insert menu to add page numbers to a document, Word automatically numbers the pages for you. ⬧ Alice adds page numbers to the bottom of each page in the document.

1. **Click Insert on the menu bar, then click Page Numbers**
   The Page Numbers dialog box opens, as shown in Figure D-7. You use this dialog box to specify the position—top or bottom of the page—and the alignment for the page numbers. Bottom of page (Footer) is the default position.

QuickTip
You can also align page numbers with the left, right, inside, or outside margins of a document.

2. **Click the Alignment list arrow, then click Center**
   The page numbers will be centered between the left and right margins at the bottom of each page.

3. **Click OK, then scroll to the bottom of the first page**
   The page number 1 appears in gray at the bottom of the first page, as shown in Figure D-8. The number is gray, or dimmed, because it is located in the Footer area. When the document is printed, the page numbers appear as normal text. You will learn more about headers and footers in the next lesson.

4. **Click the Print Preview button ⬚ on the Standard toolbar, then click the One Page button ⬚ on the Print Preview toolbar if necessary**
   The first page of the newsletter appears in Print Preview. Notice the page number.

5. **Click the page number with the ⬚ pointer to zoom in on the page**
   The page number is centered at the bottom of the page, as shown in Figure D-9.

6. **Scroll down the document to see the page number at the bottom of each page**
   Word automatically numbered the pages of the newsletter.

QuickTip
To display more than six pages of a document in Print Preview, drag to expand the Multiple Pages grid.

7. **Click the Multiple Pages button ⬚ on the Print Preview toolbar, point to the second box in the bottom row on the grid to select 2 x 2 pages, then click**
   All four pages of the newsletter appear in the Print Preview window.

8. **Click Close on the Print Preview toolbar, then save the document**

Inserting date and time fields

Using the Date and Time command on the Insert menu, you can add a field for the current date or the current time into a document. To insert the current date or time at the location of the insertion point, click Date and Time on the Insert menu, then select the date or time format you want to use from the list of available formats in the Date and Time dialog box. To insert the date or time as a field that will be updated automatically each time you open or print the document, select the Update automatically check box, then click OK. If you want to insert the current date or time as static text that does not change each time you open or print the document, deselect the Update automatically check box, then click OK. Word uses the clock on your computer to compute the current date and time.

Once you have inserted a date or time field, you can modify the format by changing the field code: right-click the field, click Edit Field on the shortcut menu, then select a new format in the Field properties list in the Field dialog box. You can edit static text just as you would any other text in Word.

Set location for page number
(header or footer)

Set alignment of page number

Clear to hide the page number
on the first page

Click to change the
numbering format

Preview of
page number
position

FIGURE D-8: **Page number in document**

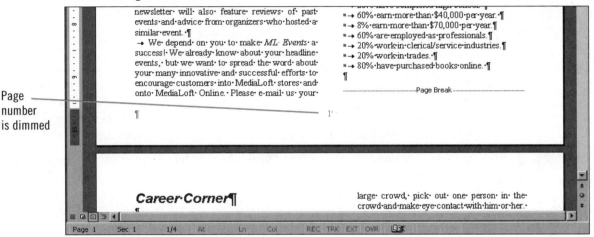

Page
number
is dimmed

FIGURE D-9: **Page number in Print Preview**

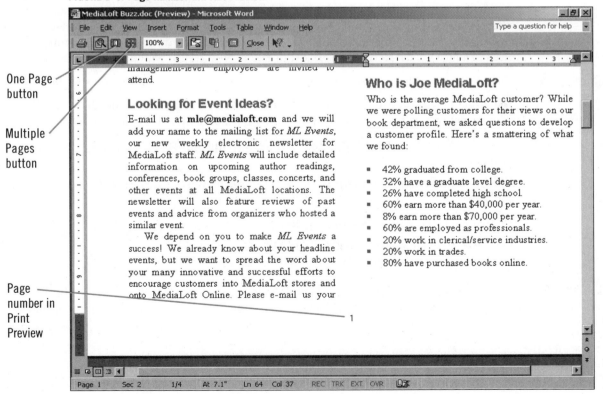

One Page
button

Multiple
Pages
button

Page
number in
Print
Preview

Inserting Headers and Footers

A **header** is text or graphics that appears at the top of every page of a document. A **footer** is text or graphics that appears at the bottom of every page. In longer documents, headers and footers often contain information such as the title of the publication, the title of the chapter, the name of the author, the date, or a page number. You can add headers and footers to a document by using the Header and Footer command on the View menu to open the Header and Footer areas, and then inserting text and graphics in them. ✒️ Alice creates a header that includes the name of the newsletter and the current date.

Steps 1 2 3 4

1. **Click View on the menu bar, then click Header and Footer**
   The Header and Footer areas open and the document text is dimmed, as shown in Figure D-10. When the document text is dimmed, it cannot be edited. The Header and Footer toolbar also opens. It includes buttons for inserting standard text into headers and footers and for navigating between headers and footers. See Table D-3. The Header and Footer areas of a document are independent of the document itself and must be formatted separately. For example, if you select all the text in a document and then change the font, the header and footer font does not change.

2. **Type Buzz in the Header area, press [Spacebar] twice, then click the Insert Date button 🗎 on the Header and Footer toolbar**
   Clicking the Insert Date button inserts a date field into the header. The date is inserted using the default date format (usually month/date/year, although your default date format might be different). The word "Buzz" and the current date will appear at the top of every page in the document.

3. **Select Buzz and the date, then click the Center button 🗎 on the Formatting toolbar**
   The text is centered in the Header area. You can also use tabs to center and right-align text in the Header and Footer areas. Notice that the center and right tab stops shown on the ruler do not align with the current margin settings. The tab stops are the default tab stops for the Header and Footer areas, based on the default margin settings. If you change the margins in a document, you need to adjust the tab stops in the Header or Footer area to align with the new margin settings.

4. **With the text still selected, click the Font list arrow on the Formatting toolbar, click Arial, click the Bold button 🗎, then click in the Header area to deselect the text**
   The header text is formatted in 12-point Arial bold, as shown in Figure D-11.

5. **Click the Switch Between Header and Footer button 🗎 on the Header and Footer toolbar**
   The insertion point moves to the Footer area. A page number field already appears centered in the Footer area.

6. **Double-click the page number to select the field, click the Font list arrow, click Arial, click 🗎, then click in the Footer area to deselect the field**
   The page number is formatted in 12-point Arial bold.

7. **Click Close on the Header and Footer toolbar, save the document, then scroll down until the bottom of page 1 and the top of page 2 appear in the document window**
   The Header and Footer areas close and the header and footer text is dimmed, as shown in Figure D-12. The header text—"Buzz" and the current date—appear at the top of every page in the document, and a page number appears at the bottom of each page.

FIGURE D-10: **Header area**

Header and Footer toolbar

Header area is open

Document text is dimmed

Insert Date button

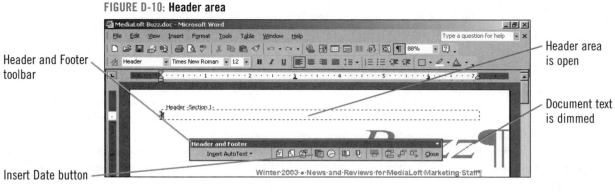

FIGURE D-11: **Formatted header text**

Information in Header area for section 1 appears on every page

Formatted text is centered in the Header area

Tab stops for the header are set for the default document margins

Switch Between Header and Footer button

FIGURE D-12: **Header and footer in the document**

Page number appears in footer on every page

Header text appears in header on every page (your date will differ)

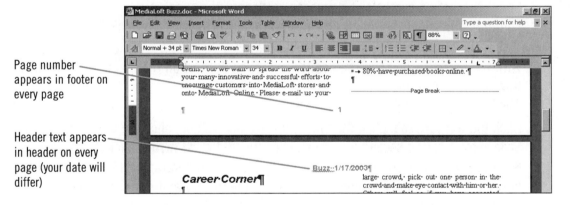

Word 2002

TABLE D-3: **Buttons on the Header and Footer toolbar**

button	function
Insert AutoText ▾	Inserts an AutoText entry, such as a field for the filename, or the author's name
⊞ Insert Page Number	Inserts a field for the page number so that the pages are numbered automatically
⊞ Insert Number of Pages	Inserts a field for the total number of pages in the document
⊞ Format Page Number	Opens the Page Number Format dialog box; use to change the numbering format or to begin automatic page numbering with a specific number
⊞ Insert Date	Inserts a field for the current date
⊘ Insert Time	Inserts a field for the current time
⊞ Page Setup	Opens the Page Setup dialog box
⊞ Switch Between Header and Footer	Moves the insertion point between the Header and Footer areas

Editing Headers and Footers

To change header and footer text or to alter the formatting of headers and footers you must first open the Header and Footer areas. You can open headers and footers using the Header and Footer command on the View menu, or by double-clicking a header or footer in Print Layout view. ✏ Alice modifies the header by adding a small circle symbol between "Buzz" and the date. She also adds a border under the header text to set it off from the rest of the page. Finally, she removes the header and footer text from the first page of the document.

Steps

1. **Place the insertion point at the top of page 2, position the ☐ pointer over the header text at the top of page 2, then double-click**
   The Header and Footer areas open.

2. **Place the insertion point between the two spaces after Buzz, click Insert on the menu bar, then click Symbol**
   The Symbol dialog box opens and is similar to Figure D-13. **Symbols** are special characters, such as graphics, shapes, and foreign language characters, that you can insert into a document. The symbols shown in Figure D-13 are the symbols included with the (normal text) font. You can use the Font list arrow on the Symbols tab to view the symbols included with each font on your computer.

3. **Scroll the list of symbols if necessary to locate the black circle symbol shown in Figure D-13, select the black circle symbol, click Insert, then click Close**
   A circle symbol is added at the location of the insertion point.

4. **With the insertion point in the header text, click Format on the menu bar, then click Borders and Shading**
   The Borders and Shading dialog box opens.

5. **Click the Borders tab, click Custom in the Setting section, click the dotted line in the Style scroll box (the second line style), click the Width list arrow, click 2¼ pt, click the Bottom border button in the Preview section, make sure Paragraph is selected in the Apply to list box, click OK, then click Close on the Header and Footer toolbar**
   A dotted line border is added below the header text, as shown in Figure D-14.

6. **Press [Ctrl][Home] to move the insertion point to the beginning of the document**
   The newsletter already includes the name of the document at the top of the first page, making the header information redundant. You can modify headers and footers so that the header and footer text does not appear on the first page of a document or a section.

7. **Click File on the menu bar, click Page Setup then click the Layout tab**
   The Layout tab of the Page Setup dialog box includes options for creating a different header and footer for the first page of a document or a section, and for creating different headers and footers for odd- and even-numbered pages in a document or a section. For example, in a document with facing pages, such as a magazine, you might want the publication title to appear in the left-page header and the publication date to appear in the right-page header.

8. **Click the Different first page check box to select it, click the Apply to list arrow, click Whole document, then click OK**
   The header and footer text is removed from the Header and Footer areas on the first page.

9. **Scroll to see the header and footer on pages 2, 3, and 4, then save the document**

FIGURE D-13: **Symbol dialog box**

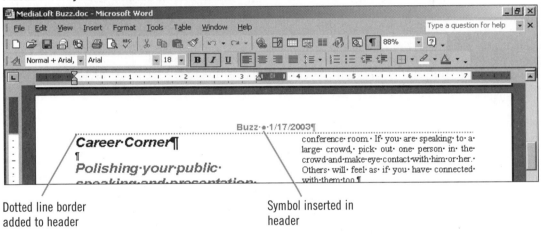

Black circle symbol is selected

Name of selected symbol

Inserts selected symbol at location of insertion point

The subset changes as you scroll the list of symbols

Available symbols (yours might differ)

Character code for selected symbol

FIGURE D-14: **Symbol and border added to header**

Dotted line border added to header

Symbol inserted in header

Inserting and creating AutoText entries

Word includes a number of built-in AutoText entries, including salutations and closings for letters, as well as information for headers and footers. To insert a built-in AutoText entry at the location of the insertion point, point to AutoText on the Insert menu, point to a category on the AutoText menu, then click the AutoText entry you want to insert. You can also use the Insert AutoText button on the Header and Footer toolbar to insert an AutoText entry from the Header/Footer category into a header or footer.

Word's AutoText feature also allows you to store text and graphics that you use frequently so that you can easily insert them in a document. To create a custom AutoText entry, enter the text or graphic you want to store—such as a company name or logo—in a document, select it, point to AutoText on the Insert menu, and then click New. In the Create AutoText dialog box, type a name for your AutoText entry, then click OK. The text or graphic is saved as a custom AutoText entry. To insert a custom AutoText entry in a document, point to AutoText on the Insert menu, click AutoText, select the entry name on the AutoText tab in the AutoCorrect dialog box, click Insert, then click OK.

Formatting Columns

Formatting text in columns often makes it easier to read. You can apply column formatting to a whole document, to a section, or to selected text. The Columns button on the Standard toolbar allows you to quickly create columns of equal width. In addition, you can use the Columns command on the Format menu to create columns and to customize the width and spacing of columns. To control the way text flows between columns, you can insert a **column break**, which forces the text following the break to move to the top of the next column. You can also balance columns of unequal length by inserting a continuous section break at the end of the last column in a section. ⚐ Alice formats the Staff News page in three columns, then she adjusts the flow of text.

Steps 1234

1. Scroll to the top of page 4, place the insertion point before **Boston**, click **Insert** on the menu bar, click **Break**, select the **Continuous option button**, then click **OK**

A continuous section break is inserted before Boston. The newsletter now contains three sections.

QuickTip

To change the width and spacing of existing columns, you can use the Columns dialog box or drag the column markers on the horizontal ruler.

2. Refer to the status bar to confirm that the insertion point is in section 3, click **Format** on the menu bar, then click **Columns**

The Columns dialog box opens, as shown in Figure D-15.

3. Select **Three** in the Presets section, click the **Spacing down arrow** twice until 0.3" appears, select the **Line between check box**, then click **OK**

All the text in section 3 is formatted in three columns of equal width with a line between the columns, as shown in Figure D-16.

QuickTip

To create a banner headline that spans the width of a page, select the headline text, click the Columns button, then click 1 Column.

4. Click the **Zoom list arrow** on the Standard toolbar, then click **Whole Page**

Notice that the third column of text is much shorter than the first two columns. Page 4 would look better if the three columns were balanced—each the same length.

5. Place the insertion point at the end of the third column, click **Insert** on the menu bar, click **Break**, select the **Continuous option button**, then click **OK**

The columns in section 3 adjust to become roughly the same length.

6. Scroll up to page 3

The two columns on page 3 are also uneven. The page would look better if the information about the third webcast did not break across the two columns.

QuickTip

If a section contains a column break, you cannot balance the columns by inserting a continuous section break.

7. Click the **Zoom list arrow**, click **Page Width**, scroll to the bottom of page 3, place the insertion point before **Tuesday, June 10**, click **Insert** on the menu bar, click **Break**, click the **Column break option button**, then click **OK**

The text following the column break is forced to the top of the next column.

8. Click the **Zoom list arrow**, click **Two Pages**, then save the document

The columns on pages 3 and 4 are displayed, as shown in Figure D-17.

CLUES TO USE

Hyphenating text in a document

Hyphenating a document is another way to control the flow of text in columns. Hyphens are small dashes that break words that fall at the end of a line. Hyphenation diminishes the gaps between words in justified text and reduces ragged right edges in left-aligned text. If a document includes narrow columns, hyphenating the text can help give the pages a cleaner look. To hyphenate a document automatically, point to Language on the Tools menu, click Hyphenation, select the Automatically hyphenate document check box in the Hyphenation dialog box, and then click OK. You can also use the Hyphenation dialog box to change the hyphenation zone—the distance between the margin and the end of the last word in the line. A smaller hyphenation zone results in a greater number of hyphenated words and a cleaner look to columns of text.

FIGURE D-15: Columns dialog box

Select a preset format for columns

Change the number of columns

Select to add a line between columns

Preview of current settings

Set custom widths and spacing for columns

Select to create columns of equal width

Select part of document to apply format to

FIGURE D-16: Text formatted in three columns

Column markers show the width and spacing of columns

Text in section 3 is formatted in 3 columns

Section break is at end of section 2

Line added between columns

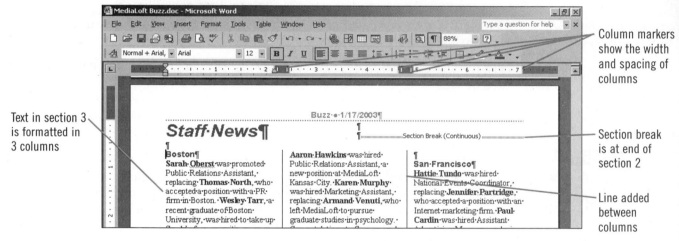

FIGURE D-17: Completed pages 3 and 4 of newsletter

Text following column break is forced to top of next column

Column break

Continuous section break

Columns in section are balanced

Inserting Clip Art

Illustrating a document with clip art images can give it visual appeal and help to communicate your ideas. **Clip art** is a collection of graphic images that you can insert into a document. Clip art images are stored in the Clip Organizer, a library of the **clips**—media files, including graphics, photographs, sounds, movies, and animations—that come with Word. Clips are organized in collections in the Clip Organizer. You can add a clip to a document using the Clip Art command on the Insert menu. Once you insert a clip art image, you can wrap text around it, resize it, and move it to a different location. ✒ Alice illustrates the second page of the newsletter with a clip art image. After she inserts the image, she wraps text around it, enlarges it, and then moves it so that it is centered between the two columns of text.

Steps

1. Click the **Zoom list arrow** on the Standard toolbar, click **Page Width**, scroll to the top of page 2, then place the insertion point before the first body paragraph, which begins **Did you know...**
   You will insert the clip art graphic at the location of the insertion point.

2. Click **Insert** on the menu bar, point to **Picture**, then click **Clip Art**
   The Insert Clip Art task pane opens, as shown in Figure D-18. You can use this task pane to search for clips related to a keyword.

   Trouble?
   If the Add Clips to Organizer message box opens, click Later.

3. Select the text in the Search text text box if necessary, type **communication**, then click **Search**
   Clips with the keyword "communication" appear in the Insert Clip Art task pane, as shown in Figure D-19. When you point to a clip, a ScreenTip showing the first few keywords applied to the clip, the width and height of the clip in pixels, and the file size and file type for the clip appears.

4. Point to the **clip** shown in Figure D-19, click the **list arrow** that appears next to the clip, click **Insert** on the menu, then close the Insert Clip Art task pane
   The clip is inserted at the location of the insertion point. You want to center the graphic on the page. Until you apply text wrapping to a graphic, it is part of the line of text in which it was inserted (an **inline graphic**). To move a graphic independently of text, you must wrap the text around it to make it a **floating graphic**, which can be moved anywhere on a page.

   Trouble?
   Select a different clip if the clip shown in Figure D-19 is not available to you.

5. Double-click the **clip art image**, click the **Layout tab** in the Format Picture dialog box, click **Tight**, then click **OK**
   The text in the first body paragraph wraps around the irregular shape of the clip art image. The white circles that appear on the square edges of the graphic are the **sizing handles**, which appear when a graphic is selected. You can drag a sizing handle to change the size of the image.

6. Position the pointer over the **lower-right sizing handle**, when the pointer changes to ↘ drag down and to the right until the graphic is about 2½" wide and 2½" tall
   As you drag a sizing handle, the dotted lines show the outline of the graphic. Refer to the dotted lines and the rulers as you resize the graphic. When you release the mouse button, the image is enlarged.

   QuickTip
   To verify the size of a graphic or to set precise measurements, double-click the graphic to open the Format Picture dialog box, then adjust the Height and Width settings on the Size tab.

7. With the graphic still selected, position the pointer over the graphic, when the pointer changes to ⇱ drag the graphic down and to the right so it is centered on the page as shown in Figure D-20, release the mouse button, then deselect the graphic
   The graphic is now centered between the two columns of text.

8. **Click the Zoom list arrow**, then click **Two Pages**
   The completed pages 1 and 2 are displayed, as shown in Figure D-21.

   Trouble?
   If page 3 is a blank page or contains text continued from page 2, reduce the size of the graphic on page 2.

9. Press **[Ctrl][End]**, press **[Enter]**, type your name, save your changes, print the document, then close the document and exit Word

FIGURE D-18: Insert Clip Art task pane

Type search keyword here

Select collections in which to search for clips

Select type of clips

Click to open the Clip Organizer

Click to search for clips online

FIGURE D-19: Clips in task pane

Click to expand display of clips

Click to begin a different search

Select this clip

Clips with the keyword "communication"

FIGURE D-20: Graphic being moved to a new location

Sizing handle

Text is wrapped around graphic

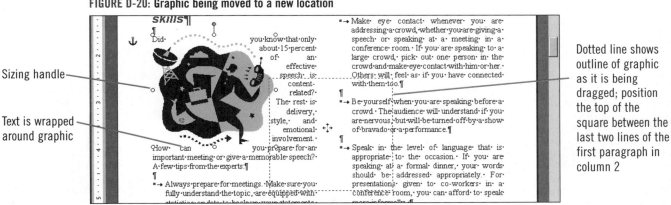

Dotted line shows outline of graphic as it is being dragged; position the top of the square between the last two lines of the first paragraph in column 2

FIGURE D-21: Completed pages 1 and 2 of newsletter

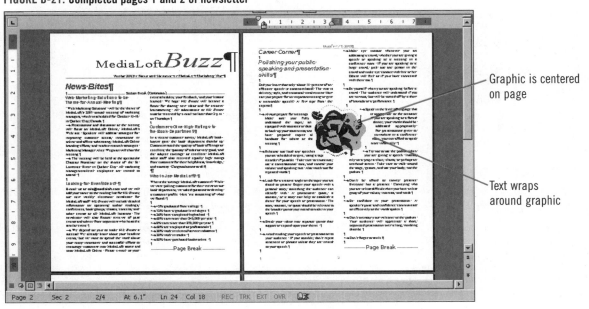

Graphic is centered on page

Text wraps around graphic

Practice

► Concepts Review

Label each element shown in Figure D-22.

FIGURE D-22

Match each term with the statement that best describes it.

7. **Section break**
8. **Header**
9. **Footer**
10. **Field**
11. **Hard page break**
12. **Margin**
13. **Inline graphic**
14. **Floating graphic**

a. A formatting mark that forces the text following the mark to begin at the top of the next page

b. The blank area between the edge of the text and the edge of the page

c. A placeholder for information that changes

d. Text or graphics that appears at the top of every page in a document

e. An image to which text wrapping has been applied

f. A formatting mark that divides a document into parts that can be formatted differently

g. An image that is inserted as part of a line of text

h. Text or graphics that appears at the bottom of every page in a document

Select the best answer from the list of choices.

15. Which of the following do documents with mirror margins always have?
a. Landscape orientation
b. Inside and outside margins
c. Gutters
d. Different first page headers and footers

16. Which button is used to insert a field into a header or footer?
a. ▣
b. ▥
c. ▨
d. ▦

17. Which type of break do you insert if you want to force text to begin on the next page?
a. Continuous section break
b. Soft page break
c. Hard page break
d. Text wrapping break

18. Which type of break do you insert if you want to balance the columns in a section?
a. Continuous section break
b. Soft page break
c. Column break
d. Text wrapping break

19. What must you do to change an inline graphic to a floating graphic?
a. Resize the graphic
b. Move the graphic
c. Apply text wrapping to the graphic
d. Anchor the graphic

20. Pressing [Ctrl][Enter] does which of the following?
a. Inserts a soft page break
b. Inserts a continuous section break
c. Moves the insertion point to the beginning of the document
d. Inserts a hard page break

► Skills Review

1. Set document margins.
a. Start Word, open the file WD D-2 from the drive and folder where your Project Files are located, then save it as **Amherst Fitness**.
b. Change the top and bottom margins to 1.2" and the left and right margins to 1".
c. Save your changes to the document.

2. Divide a document into sections.
a. Scroll down, then insert a continuous section break before the **Facilities** heading.
b. Format the text in Section 2 in two columns, then save your changes to the document.

3. Add page breaks.
a. Insert a hard page break before the heading **Welcome to the Amherst Fitness Center!**, scrolling up if necessary.
b. Scroll down and insert a hard page break before the heading **Services**.
c. Scroll down and insert a hard page break before the heading **Membership**.
d. Press [Ctrl][Home], then save your changes to the document.

4. Add page numbers.
a. Insert page numbers in the document. Center the page numbers at the bottom of the page.
b. View the page numbers on each page in Print Preview, then save your changes to the document.

5. Insert headers and footers.
a. Open the Header and Footer areas, then type your name in the Header area.
b. Press [Tab] twice, then use the Insert Date button on the Header and Footer toolbar to insert the current date.
c. On the horizontal ruler, drag the right tab stop from the 6" mark to the 6½" mark so that the date aligns with the right margin of the document.
d. Move the insertion point to the Footer area.
e. Double-click the page number to select it, then format the page number in bold italic.
f. Close headers and footers, preview the header and footer on each page in Print Preview, close Print Preview, then save your changes to the document.

6. Edit headers and footers.

    a. Open headers and footers, then apply italic to the text in the header.

    b. Move the insertion point to the Footer area, double-click the page number to select it, then press [Delete].

    c. Click the Align Right button on the Formatting toolbar.

    d. Use the Symbol command on the Insert menu to open the Symbol dialog box.

    e. Insert a black right-pointing triangle symbol, then close the Symbol dialog box.

    f. Use the Insert Page Number button on the Header and Footer toolbar to insert a page number.

    g. Use the Page Setup button on the Header and Footer toolbar to open the Page Setup dialog box.

    h. Use the Layout tab to create a different header and footer for the first page of the document.

    i. Scroll to the beginning of the document. If you want your name on the first page of the document, type your name in the First Page Header area, then apply italic to your name.

    j. Close headers and footers, preview the header and footer on each page in Print Preview, close Print Preview, then save your changes to the document.

7. Format columns.

    a. On page 2, select **Facilities** and the paragraph mark below it, use the Columns button to format the selected text as one column, then center **Facilities** on the page.

    b. Balance the columns on page 2 by inserting a continuous section break at the bottom of the second column.

    c. On page 3, select **Services** and the paragraph mark below it, format the selected text as one column, then center the text.

    d. Balance the columns on page 3.

    e. On page 4, select **Membership** and the paragraph mark below it, format the selected text as one column, then center the text.

    f. Insert a column break before the **Membership Cards** heading, then save your changes to the document.

8. Insert clip art.

    a. On page 1, place the insertion point in the second blank paragraph below **A Rehabilitation and Exercise Facility**. (*Hint*: Place the insertion point to the left of the paragraph mark.)

    b. Open the Insert Clip Art task pane. Search for clips related to the keyword **Victories**.

    c. Insert the clip shown in Figure D-23. Select a different clip if this one is not available to you.

    d. Select the graphic, then drag the lower-right sizing handle up and to the left so that the graphic is about 2" wide and 3" tall. Size the graphic so that all the text and the hard page break fit on page 1. (*Hint*: The sizing handles on inline graphics are black squares.)

    e. Scroll to page 3, then place the insertion point before the **Personal Training** heading.

    f. In the Insert Clip Art task pane, search for an appropriate clip to illustrate this page. You might try searching using the keywords **sports**, **health**, or **heart**.

    g. When you find an appropriate clip, insert it in the document, then close the Insert Clip Art task pane.

    h. Double-click the graphic to open the Format Picture dialog box, then click the Layout tab. Apply the Tight text wrapping style to the graphic.

    i. Move the graphic so that it is centered below the text at the bottom of the page (below the page break mark). Adjust the size and position of the graphic so that the page looks attractive.

    j. Save your changes to the document. Preview the document, print a copy, then close the document and exit Word.

FIGURE D-23

The Amherst Fitness Center

A Rehabilitation and Exercise Facility

Member Services

▶ Independent Challenge 1

You are the owner of a small catering business in Latona, Ontario called Bon Appetit Catering Services. You have begun work on the text for a brochure advertising your business and are now ready to lay out the pages and prepare the final copy. The brochure will be printed on both sides of an 8½" × 11" sheet of paper, and folded in thirds.

FIGURE D-24

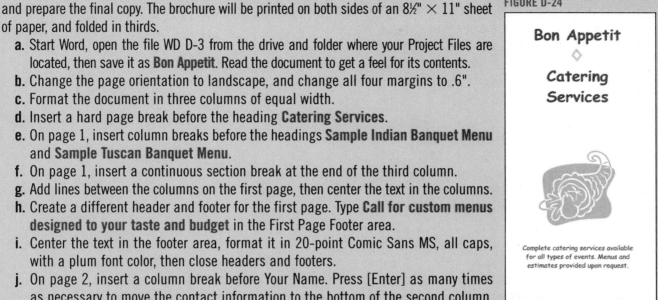

a. Start Word, open the file WD D-3 from the drive and folder where your Project Files are located, then save it as **Bon Appetit**. Read the document to get a feel for its contents.

b. Change the page orientation to landscape, and change all four margins to .6".

c. Format the document in three columns of equal width.

d. Insert a hard page break before the heading **Catering Services**.

e. On page 1, insert column breaks before the headings **Sample Indian Banquet Menu** and **Sample Tuscan Banquet Menu**.

f. On page 1, insert a continuous section break at the end of the third column.

g. Add lines between the columns on the first page, then center the text in the columns.

h. Create a different header and footer for the first page. Type **Call for custom menus designed to your taste and budget** in the First Page Footer area.

i. Center the text in the footer area, format it in 20-point Comic Sans MS, all caps, with a plum font color, then close headers and footers.

j. On page 2, insert a column break before Your Name. Press [Enter] as many times as necessary to move the contact information to the bottom of the second column. Be sure all five lines of the contact information are in column 2 and do not flow to the next column.

k. Replace Your Name with your name, then center the contact information in the column.

l. Insert a column break at the bottom of the second column. Then, type the text shown in Figure D-24 in the third column. Refer to the figure as you follow the instructions for formatting the text in the third column.

m. Format **Bon Appetit Catering Services** in 28-point Comic Sans MS, bold, with a plum font color.

n. Format the remaining text in 12-point Comic Sans MS, with a plum font color. Center the text in the third column.

o. Below Bon Appetit, insert the symbol shown in Figure D-24. (*Hint*: Type the character code 25CA in the Character code text box in the Symbol dialog box to find the symbol.) Change the font color of the symbol to gold.

p. Insert the clip art graphic shown in Figure D-24 or another appropriate clip art graphic. Do not wrap text around the graphic.

q. Add and remove blank paragraphs in the third column of your brochure so that the spacing between elements roughly matches the spacing shown in Figure D-24.

r. Save your changes, preview the brochure in Print Preview, then print a copy. If possible, print the two pages of the brochure back to back so that the brochure can be folded in thirds. Close the document and exit Word.

Word 2002

▶ Independent Challenge 2

You work in the Campus Safety Department at Miller State College. You have written the text for an informational flyer about parking regulations on campus and now you need to format the flyer so it is attractive and readable.

a. Start Word, open the file WD D-4 from the drive and folder where your Project Files are located, then save it as **Parking FAQ**. Read the document to get a feel for its contents.

b. Change all four margins to .7".

c. Insert a continuous section break before **1. May I bring a car to school?** (*Hint*: Place the insertion point before "May.")

d. Scroll down and insert a next page section break before **Sample Parking Permit**.

e. Format the text in section 2 in three columns of equal width with .3" of space between the columns.

f. Hyphenate the document using the automatic hyphenation feature. (*Hint*: If the Hyphenation feature is not installed on your computer, skip this step.)

g. Add a 3-pt dotted line bottom border to the blank paragraph under Miller State College. (*Hint*: Place the insertion point before the paragraph mark under Miller State College, then apply a bottom border to the paragraph.)

h. Add your name to the header. Right-align your name and format it in 10-point Arial.

i. Add the following text to the footer, inserting symbols between words as indicated: **Parking and Shuttle Service Office • 54 Buckley Street • Miller State College • 942-555-2227**.

j. Format the footer text in 10-point Arial Black and center it in the footer. Use a different font if Arial Black is not available to you. If necessary adjust the font and font size so that the entire address fits on one line.

k. Apply a 3-pt dotted line border above the footer text. Make sure to apply the border to the paragraph.

l. Balance the columns in section 2.

m. Add an appropriate clip art image to the upper-right corner of the document, above the border. Make sure the graphic does not obscure the border.

n. Place the insertion point on page 2 (which is section 4). Change the left and right margins in section 4 to 1". Also change the page orientation of section 4 to landscape.

o. Change the vertical alignment of section 4 to Center.

p. Save your changes, preview the flyer in Print Preview, then print a copy. If possible, print the two pages of the flyer back to back. Close the document and exit Word.

▶ Independent Challenge 3

A book publisher would like to publish an article you wrote on stormwater pollution in Australia as a chapter in a forthcoming book called *Environmental Issues for the New Millennium*. The publisher has requested that you format your article like a book chapter before submitting it for publication, and has provided you with a style sheet.

a. Start Word, open the file WD D-5 from the drive and folder where your Project Files are located, then save it as **Stormwater**.

b. Change the font of the entire document to 11-point Book Antiqua. If this font is not available to you, select a different font suitable for the pages of a book. Change the alignment to justified.

c. Change the paper size to 6" × 9".

d. Create mirror margins. (*Hint*: Use the Multiple Pages list arrow.) Change the top and bottom margins to .8", change the inside margin to .4", change the outside margin to .6", and create a .3" gutter to allow room for the book's binding.

e. Change the Zoom level to Two Pages. Create different headers and footers for odd- and even- numbered pages.

f. Change the Zoom level to Page Width. In the odd page header, type **Chapter 7**, insert a symbol of your choice, then type **Stormwater Pollution in the Fairy Creek Catchment**.

g. Format the header text in 9-point Book Antiqua italic, then right-align the text.

h. In the even page header, type your name, insert a symbol of your choice, then insert the current date. (*Hint*: Scroll down or use the Show Next button to move the insertion point to the even page header.)

i. Change the format of the date to include just the month and the year. (*Hint*: Right-click the date field, then click Edit Field.)

j. Format the header text in 9-point Book Antiqua italic. The even page header should be left-aligned.

k. Insert page numbers that are centered in the footer. Format the page number in 10-point Book Antiqua. Make sure to insert a page number field in both the odd and even page footer areas.

l. Format the page numbers so that the first page of Chapter 7 begins on page 53. (*Hint*: Select a page number field, then use the Format Page Number button.)

m. Go to the beginning of the document, press [Enter] 10 times, type **Chapter 7: Stormwater Pollution in the Fairy Creek Catchment**, press [Enter] twice, type your name, then press [Enter] twice.

n. Format the chapter title in 16-point Book Antiqua bold, format your name in 14-point Book Antiqua using small caps, then left-align the text.

o. Save your changes, preview the chapter in Print Preview, print the first three pages of the chapter, then close the document and exit Word.

 Independent Challenge 4

One of the most common opportunities to use Word's page layout features is when formatting a research paper. The format recommended by the *MLA Handbook for Writers of Research Papers*, a style guide that includes information on preparing, writing, and formatting research papers, is the standard format used by many schools, colleges, and universities. In this independent challenge, you will research the MLA (Modern Language Association) guidelines for formatting a research paper and use the guidelines you find to prepare a sample first page of a research report.

a. Start Word, open the file WD D-6 from the drive and folder where your Project Files are located, then save it as **MLA Style**. This document contains the questions you will answer about MLA style guidelines.

b. Use your favorite search engine to search the Web for information on the MLA guidelines for formatting a research report. Use the keywords **MLA Style** and **research paper format**, to conduct your search. If your search does not result in links to appropriate sources, try the following Web sites: http://webster.commnet.edu/mla.htm or www.mla.org.

c. Look for information on the proper formatting for the following aspects of a research paper: paper size, margins, title page or first page of the report, line spacing, paragraph indentation, page numbers, and works cited.

d. Type your answers to the questions in the MLA Style document, save it, print a copy, then close the document.

e. Using the information you learned, start a new document and create a sample first page of a research report. Use **MLA Format for Research Papers** as the title for your sample report, and make up information about the course and instructor, if necessary. For the body of the report, type several sentences about MLA style. Make sure to format the page exactly as the MLA style dictates.

f. Save the document as **MLA Sample Format** to the drive and folder where your Project Files are located, print a copy, close the document, then exit Word.

► Visual Workshop

Use the file WD D-7, found on the drive and folder where your Project Files are located, to create the article shown in Figure D-25. (*Hint*: Change all four margins to .6". Make the width of the first column 2.2" and the width of the second column 4.8". Format the second column with borders and shading, but take care not to apply shading to the blank paragraph before the Clean Up heading. Select a different clip if the clip shown in the figure is not available to you.) Save the document with the filename **Gardener's Corner**, then print a copy.

FIGURE D-25

GARDENER'S CORNER

Putting a Perennial Garden to Bed

By Your Name

A certain sense of peace descends when a perennial garden is put to bed for the season. The plants are safely tucked in against the elements, and the garden is ready to welcome the first signs of life. When the work is done, you can sit back and anticipate the bright blooms of spring. Many gardeners are uncertain of how to close a perennial garden. This week's column demystifies the process.

Clean up

Debris that is left on top of soil invites garden pests to lay their eggs and spend the winter. Garden clean up can be a gradual process—plants will deteriorate at different rates, allowing you to do a little bit each week.

1. Edge beds and borders and remove stakes and other plant supports.
2. Dig and divide irises, daylilies, and other early bloomers.
3. Cut back plants when foliage starts to deteriorate.
4. Rake all debris out of the garden and pull any weeds that remain.

Plant perennials

Fall is the perfect time to plant perennials! The warm, sunny days and cool nights provide optimal conditions for new root growth.

1. Dig deeply and enhance soil with organic matter.
2. Use a good starter fertilizer to speed up new root growth.
3. Untangle the roots of new plants before planting them.
4. Water deeply after planting as the weather dictates.

Add compost

Organic matter is the key ingredient to healthy soil. If you take care of the soil, your plants will become strong and disease resistant.

1. Use an iron rake to loosen the top few inches of soil.
2. Spread a one to two inch layer of compost over the entire garden.
3. Refrain from stepping on the area and compacting the soil.

To mulch or not to mulch?

Winter protection for perennial beds can only help plants survive the winter. Here's what works and what doesn't:

1. Always apply mulch after the ground is frozen.
2. Never apply generic hay because is contains billions of weed seeds. Also, whole leaves and bark mulch hold too much moisture.
3. Straw and salt marsh hay are excellent choices for mulch.

Microsoft Word 2002 MOUS Certification Objectives

Below is a list of the Microsoft Office User Specialist program objectives for the Core Word 2002 skills, showing where each MOUS objective is covered in the Lessons and Practice. This table lists the Core MOUS certification skills covered in the units in this book (Units A-D). The core skills without page references are covered in *Microsoft Office XP – Illustrated Second Course* (Units E-H). For more information on which Illustrated titles meet MOUS certification, please see the inside cover of this book.

MOUS Standardized Coding Number	Activity	Lesson page where skill is covered	Location in lesson where skill is covered	Practice
W2002-1	**Inserting and Modifying Text**			
W2002-1-1	Insert, modify and move text and symbols	WORD B-4 WORD B-5	Steps 1–8, Clues to Use Table	Skills Review Independent Challenges 1–4 Visual Workshop
		WORD B-6 WORD B-7 WORD B-8 WORD B-9 WORD B-10 WORD B-11 WORD B-14 WORD B-15	Steps 1–7 Clues to Use Steps 1–7, Clues to Use Table Steps 1–9 Clues to Use Steps 1–9 Clues to Use	
		WORD D-12 WORD D-13	Steps 2–3 Clues to Use	Skills Review Independent Challenges 2–3
W2002-1-2	Apply and modify text formats	WORD C-2 WORD C-3 WORD C-4 WORD C-5	Steps 2–9 Clues to Use Steps 1–9 Clues to Use	Skills Review Independent Challenges 1–3 Visual Workshop
W2002-1-3	Correct spelling and grammar usage	WORD B-12	Steps 1–9	Skills Review Independent Challenges 1–3 Visual Workshop
W2002-1-4	Apply font and text effects	WORD C-4	Steps 1–9, Quick Tip	Skills Review Independent Challenges 1–3 Visual Workshop
		WORD C-5 WORD C-16	Clues to Use Clues to Use	
W2002-1-5	Enter and format Date and Time	WORD D-8 WORD D-10 WORD D-11	Clues to Use Steps 2–3, Quick Tip Clues to Use	Skills Review Independent Challenge 3
W2002-1-6	Apply character styles	WORD C-4 WORD C-5 WORD C-7	Steps 1–8 Clues to Use Clues to Use	Independent Challenge 3
W2002-2	**Creating and Modifying Paragraphs**			
W2002-2-1	Modify paragraph formats	WORD C-6 WORD C-7 WORD C-8 WORD C-9 WORD C-10 WORD C-12 WORD C-16	Steps 1–9 Clues to Use Steps 1–9 Clues to Use Steps 1–9 Steps 1–6, Table Steps 1–8, Clues to Use	Skills Review Independent Challenges 1–3 Visual Workshop

MOUS Standardized Coding Number	Activity	Lesson page where skill is covered	Location in lesson where skill is covered	Practice
W2002-2-2	Set and modify tabs	WORD C-10	Steps 1–9	Skills Review Independent Challenges 1–3
W2002-2-3	Apply bullet, outline, and numbering format to paragraphs	WORD C-14 WORD C-15	Steps 1–8 Clues to Use	Skills Review Independent Challenges 1–3
W2002-2-4	Apply paragraph styles	WORD C-7	Clues to Use	Independent Challenge 3
W2002-3	**Formatting Documents**			
W2002-3-1	Create and modify a header and footer	WORD D-10 WORD D-11 WORD D-12	Steps 1–7, Quick Tips Table Steps 1–8	Skills Review Independent Challenges 1–3
W2002-3-2	Apply and modify column settings	WORD D-4 WORD D-5 WORD D-6 WORD D-14	Steps 4–5 Clues to Use Clues to Use Steps 1–8, Quick Tips	Skills Review Independent Challenges 1, 2 Visual Workshop
W2002-3-3	Modify document layout and Page Setup options	WORD D-2 WORD D-3 WORD D-4 WORD D-5 WORD D-6 WORD D-7 WORD D-8	Steps 1–8 Clues to Use Steps 1–6, Quick Tips, Table Clues to Use Steps 1–5, Clues to Use Table Steps 1–7, Quick Tip	Skills Review, Independent Challenges 1–4 Visual Workshop
W2002-3-4	Create and modify tables	WORD C-11	Clues to Use	
W2002-3-5	Preview and Print documents, envelopes, and labels	WORD A-12	Steps 1–4, 6–7	Skills Review Independent Challenges 1–4 Visual Workshop
W2002-4	**Managing Documents**			
W2002-4-1	Manage files and folders for documents	WORD B-3	Clues to Use	Independent Challenge 3
W2002-4-2	Create documents using templates	WORD B-16	Steps 1–9	Skills Review Independent Challenge 2 Visual Workshop
W2002-4-3	Save documents using different names and file formats	WORD A-10 WORD A-11 WORD B-2 WORD B-3	Steps 1–6, Clues to Use Table Steps 5–6 Clues to Use	Skills Review, Independent Challenges 1–4 Visual Workshop Skills Review Independent Challenges 1–4 Visual Workshop
W2002-5	**Working with Graphics**			
W2002-5-1	Insert images and graphics	WORD D-16	Steps 1–8	Skills Review, Independent Challenges 1, 2 Visual Workshop
W2002-5-2	Create and modify diagrams and charts			
W2002-6	**Workgroup Collaboration**			
W2002-6-1	Compare and Merge documents			
W2002-6-2	Insert, view, and edit comments			
W2002-6-3	Convert documents into Web pages			

Project Files List

Read the following information carefully!

It is very important to organize and keep track of the files you need for this book.

1. **Find out from your instructor the location of the Project Files you need and the location where you will store your files.**

   - To complete many of the units in this book, you need to use Project Files. Your instructor will either provide you with a copy of the Project Files or ask you to make your own copy.

   - If you need to make a copy of the Project Files, you will need to copy a set of files from a file server, stand-alone computer, or the Web to the drive and folder where you will be storing your Project Files.

   - Your instructor will tell you which computer, drive letter, and folders contain the files you need, and where you will store your files.

   - You can also download the files by going to www.course.com. See the inside back cover of the book for instructions on how to download your files.

2. **Copy and organize your Project Files.**

   ### Floppy disk users

   - If you are using floppy disks to store your Project Files, the list on the following pages shows which files you'll need to copy onto your disk(s).

   - Unless noted in the Project Files List, you will need one formatted, high-density disk for each unit. For each unit you are assigned, copy the files listed in the **Project File Supplied column** onto one disk.

   - Make sure you label each disk clearly with the unit name (e.g., Word Unit A).

   - When working through the unit, save all your files to this disk.

   ### Users storing files in other locations

   - If you are using a zip drive, network folder, hard drive, or other storage device, use the Project Files List to organize your files.

   - Create a subfolder for each unit in the location where you are storing your files, and name it according to the unit title (e.g., Word Unit A).

   - For each unit you are assigned, copy the files listed in the **Project File Supplied column** into that unit's folder.

   - Store the files you modify or create for each unit in the unit folder.

3. **Find and keep track of your Project Files and completed files.**

   - Use the **Project File Supplied column** to make sure you have the files you need before starting the unit or exercise indicated in the **Unit and Location column**.

   - Use the **Student Saves File As column** to find out the filename you use when saving your changes to a Project File that was provided.

   - Use the **Student Creates File column** to find out the filename you use when saving a file you create new for the exercise.

Unit and Location	Project File Supplied	Student Saves File As	Student Creates File
Word Unit A			
Lessons			Marketing Memo.doc
Skills Review			Lacasse Fax.doc
Independent Challenge 1			Zobel Letter.doc
Independent Challenge 2			Smart Tags Memo.doc
Independent Challenge 3			Komata Letter.doc
Independent Challenge 4			Business Letters.doc
Visual Workshop			Publishing Cover Letter.doc
Word Unit B			
Lessons	WD B-1.doc	NY Press Release.doc	
			NYT Fax.doc
Skills Review	WD B-2.doc	CAOS Press Release.doc	
			CAOS Fax.doc
Independent Challenge 1	WD B-3.doc	Lyric Theatre Letter.doc	
Independent Challenge 2			Global Dynamics Letter.doc
Independent Challenge 3	WD B-4.doc	Computer Memo.doc	
Independent Challenge 4	WD B-5.doc	Web References.doc	
Visual Workshop			Visa Letter.doc
Word Unit C			
Lessons	WD C-1.doc	Chicago Marketing Report.doc	
Skills Review	WD C-2.doc	EDA Report.doc	
Independent Challenge 1	WD C-3.doc	Zakia Construction.doc	
Independent Challenge 2	WD C-4.doc	Membership Flyer.doc	
Independent Challenge 3	WD C-5.doc	Solstice Memo.doc	
Independent Challenge 4	WD C-6.doc	Fonts.doc	
Visual Workshop	WD C-7.doc	Rosebud Specials.doc	
Word Unit D			
Lessons	WD D-1.doc	MediaLoft Buzz.doc	
Skills Review	WD D-2.doc	Amherst Fitness.doc	
Independent Challenge 1	WD D-3.doc	Bon Appetit.doc	
Independent Challenge 2	WD D-4.doc	Parking FAQ.doc	
Independent Challenge 3	WD D-5.doc	Stormwater.doc	
Independent Challenge 4	WD D-6.doc	MLA Style.doc	
			MLA Sample Format.doc
Visual Workshop	WD D-7.doc	Gardener's Corner.doc	

Alignment   The position of text in a document relative to the margins.

Application   See *Program.*

Ask a Question box   The list box at the right end of the menu bar in which you can type or select questions for the Help system.

AutoComplete   A feature that automatically suggests text to insert.

AutoCorrect   A feature that automatically detects and corrects typing errors, minor spelling errors, and capitalization, and inserts certain typographical symbols as you type.

AutoText   A feature that stores frequently used text and graphics so they can be easily inserted into a document.

Bold   Formatting applied to text to make it thicker and darker.

Border   Lines that can be added above, below, or to the sides of paragraphs, text, and table cells.

Bullet   A small graphic symbol used to identify items in a list.

Center   Alignment in which an item is centered between the margins.

Character spacing   Formatting that changes the width or scale of characters, expands or condenses the amount of space between characters, raises or lowers characters relative to the line of text, and adjusts kerning (the space between standard combinations of letters).

Character style   A named set of character format settings that can be applied to text to format it all at once.

Click and Type pointer   A pointer used to move the insertion point and automatically apply the paragraph formatting necessary to insert text at that location in the document.

Clip art   A collection of graphic images that can be inserted into documents, presentations, Web pages, spreadsheets, and other Office files.

Clipboard   A temporary storage area for items that are cut or copied from any Office file and are available for pasting. See *Office Clipboard* and *System Clipboard.*

Column break   A break that forces text following the break to begin at the top of the next column.

Copy   To place a copy of an item on the Clipboard without removing it from a document.

Cut   To remove an item from a document and place it on the Clipboard.

Cut and paste   To move text or graphics using the Cut and Paste commands.

Delete   To permanently remove an item from a document.

Dialog box   A window that opens when a program needs more information to carry out a command.

Document   The electronic file you create using Word.

Document window   The workspace in the program window that displays the current document.

Field   A code that serves as a placeholder for data that changes in a document, such as a page number.

File   An electronic collection of information that has a unique name, distinguishing it from other files.

Filename   The name given to a document when it is saved.

First line indent   A type of indent in which the first line of a paragraph is indented more than the subsequent lines.

Floating graphic   A graphic to which text wrapping has been applied.

Font   The typeface or design of a set of characters (letters, numbers, symbols, and punctuation marks).

Font effects   Font formatting that applies special effects to text, such as shadow, outline, small caps, or superscript.

Font size   The size of characters, measured in points (pts).

Footer   Text or graphics that appears at the bottom of every page in a document or a section.

Format Painter   A feature used to copy the format settings applied to text to other text.

Formatting marks   Nonprinting characters that appear on-screen to indicate the ends of paragraphs, tabs, and other formatting elements.

Formatting toolbar   A toolbar that contains buttons for frequently used formatting commands.

Gutter   Extra margin space left for a binding at the top or left side of a document.

Hanging indent   A type of indent in which the second and subsequent lines of a paragraph are indented more than the first.

Hard page break   A page break inserted to force the text following the break to begin at the top of the next page.

Header   Text or graphics that appears at the top of every page in a document or a section.

Highlighting   Transparent color that can be applied to text to call attention to it.

Horizontal ruler   A ruler that appears at the top of the document window in Print Layout, Normal, and Web Layout view.

Hyperlink   Text or a graphic that opens a file, Web page, or other item when clicked. Also known as a link.

I-beam pointer   The I pointer, used to move the insertion point and select text.

Indent   The space between the edge of a line of text or a paragraph and the margin.

Indent markers   Markers on the horizontal ruler that show the indent settings for the active paragraph.

Inline graphic   A graphic that is part of a line of text.

Insertion point   The blinking vertical line that shows where text will appear when you type in a document.

Italic   Formatting applied to text to make the characters slanted.

Justify   Alignment in which an item is flush with both the left and right margins.

Keyboard shortcut   A combination of keys or a function key that can be pressed to perform a command.

Landscape orientation   Page orientation in which the page is wider than it is tall.

Left-align   Alignment in which the item is flush with the left margin.

Left indent   A type of indent in which the left edge of a paragraph is moved in from the left margin.

Line spacing   The amount of space between lines of text.

Margin   The blank area between the edge of the text and the edge of a page.

Menu bar   The bar beneath the title bar that contains the names of menus, that when clicked, open menus from which you can choose program commands.

Mirror margins   Margins used in documents with facing pages, where the inside and outside margins are mirror images of each other.

Negative indent A type of indent in which the left edge of a paragraph is moved to the left of the left margin.

New Document task pane A task pane that contains shortcuts for opening documents and for creating new documents.

Normal view A view that shows a document without margins, headers and footers, or graphics.

Office Assistant An animated character that appears to offer tips, answer questions, and provide access to the program's Help system.

Office Clipboard A temporary storage area shared by all Office programs that can be used to cut, copy and paste multiple items within and between Office programs. The Office Clipboard can hold up to 24 items collected from any Office program. See also *System Clipboard*.

Open To use one of the methods for opening a document to retrieve it and display it in the document window.

Outline view A view that shows the headings of a document organized as an outline.

Overtype mode A feature that allows you to overwrite existing text as you type.

Paragraph spacing The amount of space between paragraphs.

Paragraph style A named set of paragraph and character format settings that can be applied to a paragraph to format it all at once.

Paste To insert items stored on the Clipboard into a document.

Point The unit of measurement for text characters and the space between paragraphs and characters; $1/72$ of an inch.

Portrait orientation Page orientation in which the page is taller than it is wide.

Print Layout view A view that shows a document as it will look on a printed page.

Print Preview A view of a file as it will appear when printed.

Program Task-oriented software (such as Excel or Word) that enables you to perform a certain type of task such as data calculation or word processing.

Reset usage data An option that allows adapted toolbars and menus to be returned to their default settings.

Right-align Alignment in which an item is flush with the right margin.

Right indent A type of indent in which the right edge of a paragraph is moved in from the right margin.

Sans serif font A font whose characters do not include serifs, such as Arial.

Save To store a file permanently on a disk or to overwrite the copy of a file that is stored on a disk with the changes made to the file.

Save As Command used to save a file for the first time or to create a new file with a different filename, leaving the original file intact.

ScreenTip A label that appears on the screen to identify a button or to provide information about a feature.

Scroll To use the scroll bars or the arrow keys to display different parts of a document in the document window.

Scroll arrows The arrows at the ends of the scroll bars that are clicked to scroll a document one line at a time.

Scroll bars The bars on the right and bottom edges of the document window that are used to display different parts of the document in the document window.

Scroll box The box in the scroll bars that can be dragged to scroll a document.

Section A portion of a document that is separated from the rest of the document by section breaks.

Section break A formatting mark inserted to divide a document into sections.

Select To click or highlight an item in order to perform some action on it.

Serif font A font whose characters include serifs—small strokes—at the ends, such as Times New Roman.

Shading A background color or pattern that can be applied to text, tables, or graphics.

Shortcut key See *Keyboard shortcut*.

Sizing handles The black squares or white circles that appear around a graphic when it is selected; used to change the size or shape of a graphic.

Smart tag A purple dotted line that appears under text that Word identifies as a date, name, address, or place.

Smart Tag Actions button The button that appears when you point to a smart tag.

Soft page break A page break that is inserted automatically at the bottom of a page.

Standard toolbar A toolbar that contains buttons frequently used for operating and editing commands.

Status bar The bar at the bottom of the Word window that shows the vertical position, section, and page number of the insertion point, the total number of pages in a document, and the on/off status of several Word features.

Style A named collection of character and paragraph formats that are stored together and can be applied to text to format it quickly.

Subscript A font effect in which text is formatted in a smaller font size and placed below the line of text.

Superscript A font effect in which text is formatted in a smaller font size and placed above the line of text.

Symbols Special characters that can be inserted into a document using the Symbol command.

System Clipboard A clipboard that stores only the last item cut or copied from a document.

Tab See *Tab stop*.

Tab leaders Lines that appear in front of tabbed text.

Tab stop A location on the horizontal ruler that indicates where to align text.

Template A formatted document that contains placeholder text you can replace with your own text.

Title bar The bar at the top of the program window that indicates the program name and the name of the current file.

Toggle button A button that turns a feature on and off.

Toolbar A bar that contains buttons that you can click to perform commands.

Undo To reverse a change by using the Undo button or command.

Vertical alignment The position of text in a document relative to the top and bottom margins.

Vertical ruler A ruler that appears on the left side of the document window in Print Layout view.

View A way of displaying a document in the document window; each view provides features useful for editing and formatting different types of documents.

View buttons Buttons on the horizontal scroll bar that are used to change views.

Web Layout view A view that shows a document as it will look when viewed with a Web browser.

Wizard An interactive set of dialog boxes that guides you through a task.

Word processing program A software program that includes tools for entering, editing, and formatting text and graphics.

Word program window The window that contains the Word program elements, including the document window, toolbars, menu bar, and status bar.

Word wrap A feature that automatically moves the insertion point to the next line as you type.

Index

Index